UNNATURAL ENEMIES

An introduction to science and Christianity

by Kirsten Birkett

MATTHIAS MEDIA

Sydney • London

Unnatural Enemies
© Matthias Media 1997

St Matthias Press Ltd ACN 067 558 365
PO Box 225, Kingsford, NSW 2032
AUSTRALIA
Ph (02) 9663 1478; Fax (02) 9662 4289
International Ph +61-2-9663 1478; Fax +61-2-9662 4289
E-mail: matmedia@ozemail.com.au
Internet: http://www.gospelnet.com.au/matmedia/

St Matthias Press
PO Box 665, London, SW20 8RL
ENGLAND
Ph (081) 947 5686; Fax (081) 944 7091

ISBN 1 876326 01 8

Cover design & typesetting by Joy Lankshear Design P/L

Contents

Preface

Perhaps the strangest thing about university courses on the history of science is how much time they spend discussing Christianity. It was certainly so in the classes I attended, and for one important reason: many of the scientists of previous centuries were Christian believers.

As good history students, we looked for explanations for this remarkable occurrence. Indeed, many of my fellow-students found it quite odd; how could it be that for these famous men from history, their religion and their science were in such harmony? What sociological pressures could explain it?

The question had to be asked, for in our society it seems to be a strange combination. Religion and science are seen as competing explanations for the world—how can you have both? Surely the whole of history has shown the conflict between these two systems of thought. So when we come across individual scientists who also seem to take their religion seriously, we are puzzled. How can that be?

In one sense, the relationship between science and religion is a perennial question. Humans tend to be interested in how the world around them works, and they have also for a long time been interested in how they relate to God. This book is about one particular way of investigating how the world works—modern science—and one particular religion—biblical Christianity. We will look at each of them in turn, and try to gain a clearer understanding of what they are essentially about—for both are often distorted in popular discussion. We will also investigate why the two are so often portrayed as being in conflict, and to what extent this is an accurate portrayal.

This is not a technical book. It does not try to cover the subtleties of academic debate, but rather to provide an introduction to the topic for those who might be confused about how science and Christianity might operate successfully in the same world. Anyone interested in the more complex aspects of the philosophy of science or biblical theology will find avenues for further reading in the bibliography. In this book, I take an overview of the whole subject. For that reason, a lot of discussion has necessarily been left out, but hopefully what remains is still a clear summary of the issues. The aim is to help readers construct a simple framework for understanding science and the Bible.

One of the advantages of this approach is that we have become very specialised in our society. Even in high school, we have already made choices about what areas of knowledge we will study; and if we continue on to university and beyond, those areas will become increasingly narrow. It is very difficult to know much about more than one subject. Indeed, it is deceptively easy to become locked into one area of knowledge and so have a very distorted idea of others.

A topic like the relationship between science and Christianity, however, requires that we know and understand more than one subject. It requires an understanding of science—and not just particular scientific facts, but an understanding of how science as an enterprise works. It also requires an understanding of the Bible. Few people know either well, and those who do rarely understand both.

Whether I have succeeded, the reader will have to judge. To the extent that I have, I owe a debt to those who taught me both the history and philosophy of science (through my studies at the University of NSW) and the Bible (through my years at the UNSW University Church and Campus Bible Study).

In particular, I would like to acknowledge the indispensable help of Phillip Jensen, Anglican Chaplain at UNSW, and Tony Payne, Senior Editor at Matthias Media, for their input into this book. Thanks are also due to Professor Randall Albury, UNSW, for his insightful comments on the history and philosophy of science, and Drs Ross McKenzie and Lewis Jones of the Physics School at UNSW for reading the science sections. Thanks, too, to Rev. Perry Wiles of Moore Theological College who read the entire text. To all these people I am grateful, and I hope that I have faithfully represented their wisdom.

Kirsten Birkett
OCTOBER, 1997

Part I
SCIENCE

From the android Data on *Star Trek* to the dazzling redhead who rescues a baby Tyrannosaurus Rex, from the bush-trekking television naturalist to the nameless people in white coats who stand behind men or women advertising everything from washing powder to face cream, we are bombarded with images of scientists which range from the adventurous to the incomprehensible. We learned from the movie *Twister* that people with corporate sponsorship are not doing real science, and that you need to have instinct, not just instruments, to do science well. The scientists who produce the perfect hair shampoo, however, seem to spend all their time peering down microscopes. We are told that science is based on facts, science will solve all our problems, science is evil and destroys nature, science is good but the institutions which use it are evil, science is dehumanising, science is fun, science closes the mind to deeper realities, and science gives us the truth. Of all these impressions, which are real?

We begin our study by looking at science. Doing so may not be as easy as it seems. For those with little scientific background, all this material might be new and fairly challenging. Those with some scientific training, on the other hand, might feel that they are in no need of an introduction to science. However for the sake of the exercise if nothing else, both types of readers should persevere, for our society presents many different views of science, some of them quite inaccurate. We gain impressions of what science is from high school lessons, from advertisements claiming that "science proves...", from dramatic presentations of scientists in movies and television serials, and from popular writing on science. This can produce a confusing and inconsistent medley of images, and some of these images are only very loosely connected to what real scientists are like and what real scientists do.

At one level, we need to familiarise ourselves with the different terms used, so we have a common basis for discussion. More importantly, however, we need to gain an understanding of what this vast creature called 'science' is. Science has a multifaceted, complex existence in our culture, and is actually not just one entity which can be simply described. It is not surprising we have so many images of science; it is a globe-spanning organization, a way of thinking, and an enterprise which has radically altered, perhaps even created, our modern Western culture. Does that sound daunting? Let us tackle the creature, and see if we can make sense of it.

CHAPTER 1

Where did science come from?

To begin to understand science, we need to journey back a few hundred years, to when 'modern science' as we know it, began. This excursion into history may seem an odd place to start, but when we see how modern science began we are in a much better position to understand what it is now.

Humans have been investigating their world and devising theories to explain how it works for as long as recorded history. Detailed astronomical observation is recorded in ancient Babylon, and theories of the basic structure of matter are discussed in some of the oldest Greek writings. Physics is as old as Aristotle, one of the most influential theorists of all time, and Hippocratic medicine based on clinical observation flourished from around 500 BC. Moreover, in the West throughout the Middle Ages (even the so-called 'Dark' Ages), people continued to analyse the physical world and come up with theories about it.

For these reasons, it is difficult, and almost arbitrary,

to name an historical starting point for the enterprise now known as science, and whether or not this can be done at all still forms a topic for debate. Nevertheless, if any time in Western history is to be named, the seventeenth century is a good contender. Apart from numerous significant scientific discoveries, the way in which intellectuals *thought about* science began to change. The methodology that we recognize as 'science' began to emerge.

What caused these changes is hard to say; in fact, it is probably naive to talk about a definitive cause for a general intellectual movement. Various things were happening in Western society which affected the way people reasoned about the world. The Renaissance, the 'rebirth' in learning which ended the Middle Ages in Europe, stimulated interest in looking back to the original sources of ancient texts rather than the accumulated commentaries of centuries. Humanism, part of this new interest in returning to the pure sources, emphasized the need for better language studies and less obscure philosophy. The Protestant Reformation shook authority structures, as well as emphasizing the need to look into the original Bible texts. These trends encouraged searching out the original for oneself rather than relying upon traditional wisdom. Changes in society and industry also had their effect—increased urbanization, greater exploration and trade and so the 'opening up' of the world, improvements in technology, and the invention of the printing press which greatly improved dissemination of knowledge. All these factors together produced fertile soil for scientific innovation in the seventeenth century.

What were these innovations? In practical terms many of the branches of modern science began or received great boosts in this period. Copernicus developed a model of the universe in which the earth orbited the sun, rather than the other way around. Galileo, building on this, developed a mathematical physics which challenged the old medieval ideas. This new model with a moving earth is probably the most famous achievement of the 'Scientific Revolution', but other areas had discoveries just as innovative. William Harvey (1578-1657) discovered the circulation of the blood; the botanist John Ray (1627-1705) carried out vast studies in plant life.

New scientific instruments were very important in this changing study of the world. One was the telescope, which became crucial in Galileo's study of the stars. It enabled him to see such things as the moons around Jupiter, which proved that not everything revolves around the earth—an important step in establishing that the earth itself in fact revolves around the sun. Another innovative instrument was the microscope. It opened up whole new worlds of investigation, bringing the astonishing intricacy of minute objects into view. These two—the microscope and telescope—extended the human senses, so what was previously too small or too far away to be seen by the naked eye could now be examined.

A third significant new instrument, however, was of a different kind. It was the barometer, which measures air pressure. It was significant because it measured something which human senses could not possibly measure, even in principle. It was not just an extension of human senses in the way that the microscope or telescope were. With the barometer, science was now relying on a machine to do the measuring for us.

As well as this, the foundations of modern science were laid in the sense that a great deal of thought went into discovering the best *method* for finding out true information about the world. One of the most influential writers was Francis Bacon, who is famous (in this respect) for proclaiming a new age of knowledge, set free from the shackles of medieval philosophy. Knowledge was no longer to come from acceptance of ancient authority, but was to be based solidly on data from the real world. This is known generally as 'empiricism'—the idea that true knowledge comes from our senses, in observing and experimenting with the world. It is the philosophy that still dominates popular writing about science, and which is frequently championed by practising scientists. To acquire knowledge, according to Bacon, was to begin with collecting large amounts of data from observation of the world. Then, the scientist was to search for the cause of the phenomena he had observed, eliminating possible causes in a systematic manner and coming to a guess, or hypothesis (though this was not the language Bacon used) of the cause of the observed phenomena. Then the consequences of this guess were to be tested against new data. Over and above this, hypotheses themselves could be explained by more general statements or laws, and so a whole system of knowledge could be built up, with solid observational data as its base.

Bacon also proclaimed the idea that the purpose of scientific knowledge was to control the world: 'knowledge is power' was one of his most famous aphorisms. Bacon's ideas about science were formed in a broader context than mere philosophical musing about knowledge. Science was not to be the activity of an isolated individual conducting private research; rather, Bacon envisaged a (government-funded) society devoted to the pursuit of knowledge which would be used for the good of humankind. This society was to be equipped with laboratories, preparation houses, observation towers and so on, as well as the latest in scientific instruments. Labour was to be divided between scientists, some gathering foreign information, some devising experiments, others carrying out experiments and collating results, others interpreting results and deriving truths. Research was to be carried out into a vast range of areas—plants, animals, disease, astronomy, weather; and also into 'mechanical arts', such as cements for porcelain, the production of metals and so on. It is significant that Bacon proposed scientific publication, so that everyone could be aware of new and profitable inventions and the progress of science. There was to be free exchange of information internationally.

In fact, the Royal Society of London, set up in 1662 and still one of the most prestigious scientific societies, looked remarkably like Bacon's ideal scientific society—sometimes self-consciously so. Although there were some significant differences—while the Royal Society carried the King's name, it was privately funded and relied on the initiative of its members to carry out research—the new society clearly had Bacon's precepts in mind in its charter. The Royal Society took on a wide range of experimentation, in pure research as well as applications which would bring tangible benefit to humankind, and set up a tradition of scientific publication which has proved vastly influential in the development of science. Its *Philosophical Transactions* reported experiments and discoveries of the Society, as well as letters from scientists around the world, thus constituting a medium for debate amongst scientists. The Society also took upon itself the publication of scientific books by its members.

Perhaps even more profoundly, however, the Royal Society took up Bacon's philosophy of science, basing knowledge on systematic experimentation done by research committees.[1] Facts were to come first; theories were to be derived strictly from the facts. The Royal Society also specifically dismissed relying on ancient authority, following Bacon's insistence that science based on 'opinion and dogma' is useless. (It is remarkable how much of Bacon's rhetoric is echoed in the apologists of science today.)

One of the most important innovations of this period was the *mathematization of nature*. Galileo, influenced by Archimedes, was one of the first proponents of this new aspect of scientific reasoning (it does not appear in Bacon's work at all). Basically, it was the discovery that

---

1. This was the plan; in practice, as it turned out, those who actually did the experiments were largely those who had the private means to do so.

natural events and phenomena could be accurately described using mathematical equations. For example, when an object is thrown, its arc can be mathematically described as a parabola with certain characteristics. Putting physical problems into mathematical terms in this way gave a basis not only for describing nature, but also for predicting a testable conclusion. This was an enormous step forward.

It should be noted that this method rests on the assumption both that mathematical formulations are an appropriate way to encapsulate real behaviour, as well as the assumption that there is one (and *only* one) mathematical formula which truly fits the behaviour. Both of these assumptions are problematical, but the method proved remarkably successful all the same.

It was accompanied by what might be called the *mechanization of nature.* In the new methodology taken up by the Royal Society, phenomena were to be explained by some underlying mechanism. Not only was it assumed that there would be a mechanism, but that this sort of explanation was the most intelligible. That is, it was argued that if you can explain the inner mechanism of something, you understand why it acts the way it does—just as to understand a clock, you study its inner cogs and springs. An explanation in formal mechanical terms is just the sort that lends itself to mathematization, and so the two worked together to form the new philosophy.

Isaac Newton managed to give a mathematical basis to mechanics in astronomy using principles that could apply to any moving body anywhere, demonstrating the extraordinary power of this way of proceeding. He was able to explain a vast range of phenomena in simple, consistent, mathematical terms. By the end of the seventeenth century, the ideals espoused by scientists and theorists, as well as the working models that had proved so successful, had established the boundaries of what we generally recognize as modern science.

We have inherited, then, this thing known as 'science'. Now that we have it, what is it exactly? Or what has it become? Is it something you do, or should we primarily think of it as a body of knowledge? Is it defined by the people who do it, or by the way they look at the world?

We will see that the word 'science' is used in all of these ways, which can make it a rather confusing word to discuss; and indeed, this confusion has lead to some of the difficulties in discussing the relationship between science and religion. Let us now try to separate out some of these different meanings of 'science'.

CHAPTER 2
Science in practice

SCIENCE AS A METHOD

Ask someone what 'science' is, and they will probably think of what is done by highly-trained specialists in laboratories, carrying out carefully observed experiments, repeating them many times to be sure of results, and coming to certain conclusions. "Scientific tests have shown" is a very powerful phrase in our society.

Nevertheless, even a short survey of what scientists do shows how easy it is to over-simplify the picture. The word 'science' actually covers a vast range of activities, some of which seem to have very little in common. Abstruse speculation about imaginary time, for instance, is rather different from a chemical experiment in a test-tube. Biological investigation of physiological function is different from mathematical modelling of ocean currents. Observing the behaviour of a supernova is not much like observing the behaviour of a gorilla. Even the theories of science can have very different forms. A theory in quantum physics may consist mostly of mathematical symbols which are used to describe the activity of particles so small, and so strange, as to be almost beyond imagination. A theory in medical research may speak of the factors by which a disease is transmitted between people. A theory in astronomy may concern the chemical composition of a distant star. A theory in palaeontology may speculate on the muscle structure of a creature only known by fragmentary fossils of bones. Somehow, all these different activities are to be understood as being, at some basic level, the same thing.

Let us begin with the popular view, that science consists of collecting facts in the laboratory and testing theories in experiments. If you have done science at school, you will be familiar with mixing chemicals in beakers, heating things with bunsen burners and perhaps even dissecting small animals and looking at slides under microscopes. On a more sophisticated level, a lot of science is done this way—making careful, repeated observations in a laboratory. The scientist will try to develop some theory that explains the things observed in the laboratory. It might be a theory about the genetic structure of a particular animal; or about the chemical composition of a substance; or about the behaviour of sub-atomic particles. Whatever its type, a good theory should be based on a large number of observations, under different conditions, eliminating extraneous factors; and furthermore, it should make predictions which might be tested. It is derived from experience, and it is tested against the real world. In this way, the scientific theory is meant to be 'objective', by which people generally mean it is true regardless of who makes the observations, where they are, and whether or not they believe the stated result would occur.

Not all sciences follow this laboratory-based model, however. In some sciences the observations are made in the field during long-term studies—for instance, ecological studies of how a particular group of plants changes under certain environmental conditions. In zoology, studies of animal behaviour might involve watching individual animals or colonies and recording their actions and responses, or tagging animals to trace their movements. Astronomers may have to travel to visit high-powered telescopes, where they spend time taking hundreds of photographs of the sky. A meteorologist might set up instruments to measure atmospheric pressure, wind speeds, and temperature.

In each of these cases, the scientists will eventually end up in their offices—science is never purely fieldwork. Data collected in the field needs to be analysed, and sorted into what is relevant and what is not. Scientists will often spend a lot of time in front of their computers, analysing the data, testing to see if any interesting correlations can be found, making statistical analyses and so on. The ecologist might wonder how many plants of a certain species have survived in this test site as compared to another site somewhere else. The zoologist might plot the migratory patterns of a species and compare it to past years. The astronomer might compare the amount of iron in one galaxy to another. The meteorologist might be trying to design a computer model of a weather system.

Then there are the historical sciences, which study

events which happened in the past, and so are not repeatable. Geology, for instance, may present theories about how certain structures of the earth came to be the way they are. Cosmologists who study the beginning of the universe try to build a model that will account for the way they observe the universe to be now. Archaeologists carefully excavate ancient sites and study the remains of early human civilization. Historical sciences piece together what happened in the past, and how things came to be the way they are now, through building up scenarios that might explain the evidence that survives.

Why are all these different activities grouped together as a 'scientific' way of gaining knowledge? The underlying idea which is meant to be the basis of all these sciences is *empiricism*—the same ideal that motivated Bacon back in the seventeenth century. That is, in all these activities, information is gathered by looking at how the world works, and then checked again to see if the world is working the way we predict it should. Whether this takes place in the highly artificial environment of the laboratory, or by getting very dirty in the middle of a chimpanzee colony, the uniting ideal is that the data comes from the real world. We do not assume that the world must be a certain way; we check to find out. What we believe about the way in which the world works is to be based on the evidence, not just on our assumptions. Science is investigation of nature, in a highly organized and thorough way. In this sense, science is a *method* of finding out things; a method which involves testing ideas of what might be the case against the actual data.

THE LIMITATIONS OF SCIENTIFIC METHOD

Science rests on the empirical method; its theories are tested against what we experience with our senses. This is the high ideal of science, and the reason why people have confidence in it. However we must not over-simplify this principle. There are limitations to what an empirical method can tell us.

Consider a simple example of empirical investigation. In a laboratory, we heat a piece of copper, a piece of tin, and a piece of aluminium, and they all expand. We might then pose a theory: 'metals expand when heated'. We make the prediction: 'a piece of iron will expand when heated'; and when tested, this prediction matches what happens. We now have a good basis for this bit of knowledge. (The certainty of this knowledge would be very important when it comes to constructing bridges.)

However, as the philosopher David Hume pointed out some two hundred years ago, there is a problem with any philosophy based on drawing conclusions from individual observations. That is, how many observations are needed before you can say the conclusion is true? No matter how many you have, no matter how many tests you do, you can never be sure. The next piece of copper you heat might just conceivably shrink. Until you know everything in the universe, you cannot know for sure that some scientific theory is true. This might seem a quibbling argument; for experience shows that, even if we don't know for certain, this process has worked very well so far. Going from observations to generalities has provided a good basis for knowledge up until now.

Nevertheless, even this gives no guarantee for the knowledge; it falls into the same problem. How many times does this process need to work before we can be sure it will always work?

Another problem with this picture of science is that science never starts with simple observation. Even what we see with our eyes is affected by what we expect to see; this is why visual illusions work. Think of some of those famous drawings by M. C. Escher. Sometimes you see a staircase going up; sometimes it is going down. The 'magic eye' illusions are another case—they just look like random blobs on the page, until we focus our eyes, or unfocus them, and suddenly the muddle resolves into an image. Pictures which are carefully crafted to fool the eye show us that it is not always easy to see 'what is really there'.

When we come to detailed scientific observation, there are many more complications. Any student of biology will know that it is not at all easy to work out what you are looking at the first time you look into a microscope. Medical students need to be trained to read X-rays. Dissecting a rat can be totally confusing before you know what you are meant to see. It will not be the same observation regardless of who is making it, for some observations require a great deal of education before the person can make them. This becomes even more of an issue when what is being 'observed' is in principle not able to be seen—such as electrons. Sub-atomic particles are never really 'observed'—what is observed is the readout on some piece of equipment. What is more, the observation does not come before the theory. Even the language used to express an observation requires some theory to be in place. It is highly unlikely you will ever read a scientific paper which says 'I put the thin stick with the numbers on it in a liquid which had bubbles in it and the red stuff in the stick reached up to the 97'. The scientific statement would be, 'The water's temperature was 97 degrees Centigrade'. This simple statement of observation already presupposes theory about heat and the reliability of thermometers.

In a more general way, often a theory can survive even when the observation seems to disprove it. Scientists do not always simply accept what the data says. In practice, what do you do if the experiment fails? Does this really prove your theory was wrong? Or was your experimental technique wrong? Or was the equipment faulty? Or was one of the auxiliary hypotheses wrong?

Take a famous example from the history of science. Einstein's theory of general relativity was widely accepted before it had solid, confirming evidence. What gave the theory strong evidential support was when light was observed to bend around the sun in the way that Einstein's theory predicted. However imagine for a moment if the light had not been observed to bend. Would this have proved Einstein wrong or the theory of optics on which the measuring equipment was based? It is possible to stay with a theory, even if the experimental data is going against it at the moment—for the theory may have other strengths, such as its coherence within the mathematical framework, or its overall explanatory power.

We need to be careful, then, about claiming things such as science being objective, or giving complete certainty in knowledge. While there is good reason to have confidence in science's ability to describe the way the world works, we will never be absolutely sure. There will always be some level of doubt that the current theory is the right one. It may be very useful as explanation; it may have survived a whole battery of tests; its predictions may be fruitful and it may be providing whole new avenues for research; but one day, in some environment, it may fall down.

People have discussed other problems with relying upon experimental evidence to confirm or deny theories. For instance, what if two different theories about something both explain the data, and both make the same predictions? How can you tell which one is true? When the method rests on testing predictions against empirical data, there is no way of determining between them. You can only hope that one day, with further research, some situation will arise in which the two theories will make different predictions. However, this raises another problem for science. Even if there is only one existing theory, whose predictions fare well against tested data, how can you be sure that there is not another equally good (or better) one that has not yet been thought of? Science is limited by the ingenuity of scientists. If no-one has thought of the true theory, then no-one knows the truth. How can we ever be sure that the true theory is not out there somewhere? How can we be sure that someone will think of it?

Most working scientists get on with the job of testing the theories they have, which of course is necessary in order to proceed at all. Nonetheless, when broad sweeping claims about the scope of science are made, it pays to remember some of these problems. *At its most fundamental level, science lacks certainty in discovering knowledge.*

One obvious consequence of this needs to be pointed out: that is, certain aspects of current scientific knowledge might be wrong. It is unlikely that *all* of it is wrong, but even there we cannot be absolutely sure. After all, scientific theories come and go. There have been quite a lot of scientific theories which were successful in their day—that is, they explained the observable phenomena and made confirmed predictions—which have since been discarded. Medieval astronomy held that there were crystalline spheres carrying the planets around the earth. Medicine used to be based on four 'humours', the right balance of which ensured good health. Chemistry used to include a substance called 'phlogiston' whose effects are now explained by oxygen. Heat gain or loss was explained by a gain or loss of 'caloric', now thought not to exist. Electromagnetic waves were thought to move through the 'aether'. Because most people are not very well educated in the history of science—or only in its heroic 'successes'—it is easy to lose sight of just how often scientific theories have changed.

On the other hand, the fact that scientific theories *can* change is what gives people confidence in science as a method, and we need to keep those two things in balance. The empirical method cannot promise certainty, but its strength is in its ability to adapt to new information. If a scientist finds that the theory does not fit a new piece of experimental data, he or she can suggest a new theory which fits it better. In this way, science as a method keeps 'trying out' new ideas in an effort to find the theory which will fit best.

The word 'science', then, describes a practical procedure of developing and testing theories to see if we can work out what's going on in the world. It is a method which produces conclusions which are dependent upon reported experimental results, and these conclusions potentially have to survive a process of challenge by many different scientists. This leads us to a second meaning of 'science'.

SCIENCE AS A BODY OF KNOWLEDGE

When people speak of 'science', they also refer to the body of knowledge that is currently accepted by scientists, which has been produced by the scientific method. As we might imagine from the discussion above, it is not a uniform body of knowledge, fixed and final; it is constantly being added to and also subtracted from. Ideas are first suggested tentatively; they may be taken up and experimented with further, and gradually more and more people become convinced that a particular piece of information deserves to form part of the body of accepted knowledge. In a sense, it is not possible to 'learn science', at least not all of it, for it is an ongoing process; there will always be new discoveries, new insights and further evidence to keep up with.

There are some things which are so well-established, with so much experimental confirmation, that almost every working scientist would agree with them. These are the sort of things taught in school science lessons.

They include such things as Newton's laws of motion in non-extreme situations; the laws of thermodynamics; that organisms are made of cells; that disease spreads through bacteria; that chemical substances are made up of atoms and so on. It is unlikely that experimental evidence will overthrow these ideas, because they have so much confirming evidence for them.

There are other ideas which are slightly more controversial; that is, which have a good degree of supporting evidence, but might be open to revisions. For instance, the existence of black holes has some supporting evidence, but this is not regarded in the same way as, say, Einstein's General Theory of Relativity.

Then there are ideas which are highly speculative and unconfirmed. Different people would disagree as to what should go in this category; this is part of the problem with such ideas. For instance, Stephen Hawking's unbounded universe theory, which uses concepts such as imaginary time, is very speculative. At the moment, complexity theory, about how self-organising systems develop, is unconfirmed.

A good example of the way in which scientific discoveries can develop is the discussion about life on Mars. On 16th August, 1996, a paper was published in the journal *Science* which reported that certain chemicals, polycyclic aromatic hydrocarbons (PAHs), had been found in a meteorite in Antarctica. The meteorite was thought to have arrived from Mars about 12,000 years ago. PAHs are sometimes formed from by-products of living organisms. Certain carbonate deposits were also found in the meteorites, and these were similar in shape and chemical composition to carbonate deposits produced by some bacteria on earth.

The researchers who made these discoveries reported their results, and concluded that these things were evidence for the existence of bacterial life on early Mars. They did not say that they had discovered life on Mars, or that they had proved that there was such life, but that they had some evidence to support the proposition.

A few months later, two new papers were published concerning this evidence. They both concluded that it was more likely that the evidence did not support life on Mars; that there was a better, alternative explanation for the evidence. This was because the carbonate deposits, on further examination, were seen to be of a kind that is not known to be caused by living organisms. Also, the PAHs on the meteorite were discovered to be present in nearby Antarctic ice—the meteorite could well have picked them up in Antarctica, *after* it arrived from Mars.

This is an example of the scientific method at work, in this case proposing and then rejecting a potential piece of scientific knowledge. A theory was developed on the basis of certain empirical observations. Further tests suggested that the theory was not well-supported after all.

This example is also important because it shows how popular reporting can misrepresent the status of scientific knowledge. The newspaper headlines did not say "Polycyclic aromatic hydrocarbons may have had an ancient biological origin on Mars"; they were more along the lines of "Life found on Mars!". Discussion followed as if life *had* been discovered on Mars. For someone outside the scientific community, it is easy to get the impression that once science has discovered something, that is the end of the story—the thing has now been discovered, it is knowledge, it is fact. There is much more to it than that, however. It can be a long and arduous path for a tentative idea to reach the point where it is accepted in its scientific discipline as a well-supported part of the core, which can now be taken as established knowledge. Just because a scientist (even a famous scientist) presents a theory does not make it fact.

Scientific ideas fall along a continuum of 'certainty', and may move up or down depending on further discoveries. For an idea to make it to the most certain end of the continuum, it has to survive for a long time and have a lot of confirming evidence, as well as being a successful basis for other scientific ideas. Once a theory is that successful, it would take a lot for a rival idea to overthrow it. At the other end of the scale, however, are things that are 'on the edge', which might be good ideas, or might not be, and it is yet to be seen if they survive.

When we think of 'science', we might mean the well-established ideas we learnt in school, but there is a lot of other information out there, with varying degrees of certainty. Indeed, someone who has only done school science would probably be astonished at the range of scientific investigation. In this sense, school science can sometimes give the misleading impression that all scientific discoveries are fixed and irrefutable. The real world of science contains ideas which are much more fluid.

SCIENCE AS A COMMUNITY

So far, we have discussed 'science' as a method, and as a body of knowledge. This may seem a little abstract, but we have also seen that in another sense, what we are talking about is not abstract at all—it is a group of people. We say 'science proves'; but 'science' does not prove anything—people do. It is people who carry out experiments, who take photographs and measure things and look down microscopes; it is people who think of problems to solve, who look for the data that might be relevant to the problem and who come up with a theory that explains the data.

When people do science, they do it together. The knowledge gained through doing science is a matter of great cooperative effort. No-one starts completely from scratch; every scientist benefits from the efforts of previous generations, their triumphs and their mistakes. No one person could possible test for him or herself everything that is learnt during the course of a science degree. Most of the basic knowledge taught to scientists is taken on authority, as already established by other competent scientists. No physicist expects to have to invent calculus, or discover General Relativity.

Even on a day-to-day level, science is very much a cooperative effort. A great many scientists work in teams, all working on the same problem to come up with an answer. On a smaller scale, in universities scientists will employ research students or assistants to do particular tasks for them—solve a particular mathematical problem, or write a computer programme, or carry out a chemical experiment, or count the number of plants in a colony.

There is also cooperation on an international level, as scientists read each others' journal papers to see what others have done and so get ideas for new problems to solve. As the life on Mars study shows, different teams will examine each others' results, particularly if the finding seems especially interesting or radical for some reason, and so results are checked and counter-checked. Part of the reason that 'science' discovers so much is that so many people are involved. Of course, this means that scientists have to be able to trust each others' word that what is reported in a paper is true. This leads to procedures of 'refereeing', which means that before a paper can be published, other experts in the field have to agree that it is good research. A great deal of trust is involved in science, and scientific fraud is a serious misdemeanour which most universities and research institutes punish severely.

The fact that science is done by people gives a further perspective on the process. Scientific theories, and the experiments that test them, do not exist in a vacuum— scientists have to think them up. To understand science, then, as well as looking at the 'theoretical' aspects, we need to examine how scientists interact and come to new ideas. In the sixties, a young physicist named Thomas Kuhn asked this question, and his answer has become famous. He described science as a matter of successive 'paradigms', or general theories which scientists agree on. The paradigm is the basic theory that underlies the more specific experiments and problems that scientists work on. You might say that most people had a Newtonian paradigm until Einstein developed his theory of General

Relativity; then there was an Einsteinian paradigm.

In the 'normal' state of science, Kuhn said, the paradigm is well-established and agreed upon—that is, the community generally agrees on basic assumptions and general laws. Scientists will be involved in problem-solving: taking particular problems, and demonstrating how they can be explained in terms of the general laws. While in 'normal' science, Kuhn claimed, the paradigm is resistant to change. For instance, if a scientist claimed that he or she had suddenly proved Einstein to be wrong, most people would not take the claim very seriously. Certain sociological factors reinforce the paradigm—scientists with new theories may find it hard to get funding, or to be published—and so the paradigm remains largely unchallenged.

Some people dislike this kind of description of science, for it seems to undermine the seriousness of what scientists do. It seems to suggest that science is 'just politics', and not about making real discoveries about the world. However that is not the point of this kind of discussion. To acknowledge the forces that bear upon the people who do science is not the same as saying that science is irrational, or anything like that. While under a certain paradigm, it may be entirely rational to resist a bizarre theory which seems to go against everything already understood. We can only make decisions according to the best information we have. If all scientists were prepared to overthrow their entire framework at any time, no constructive work could be done. However, what Kuhn highlighted, and many others since, is that the body of people who do science are part of the very knowledge which we call 'scientific'. We cannot understand what science is without taking into account that it is done by people, who need to interact together in certain ways. What gets discovered is affected by who gets funding, who is taken seriously by the community, and who gets the powerful jobs. Good science has to meet certain standards; but the standards have to be set by people.

We have seen, then, that science in practice is much more complicated than one might think! It is not just a matter of men in white coats doing inexplicable things in laboratories. It is a massive engine of knowledge production, which involves people who have trained and become experts in their craft, who embark on a highly specialized activity of delving into the world. The things they find out about the world sometimes survive and become confirmed as different people test them and arrive at the same answers; sometimes they do not survive. Why does our society trust science? Because of this very process. If a piece of information has survived the rigorous interrogation of generations of scientists, then we can put a lot of confidence in such information. If it also becomes the basis for technology that we can see working every day—televisions, computers, telephones, aeroplanes— then our confidence is increased. What it sets out to do, science generally does well.

We have not yet, however, exhausted the meanings that the word 'science' has. For because of its very success in *doing*, science has taken on a significance in our culture which makes it more than just an activity.

A shift has taken place, such that when people speak of science they do not necessarily mean a process of finding things out; they can mean something much more grand. 'Science' has grown out of its historical place as an activity or *practice* to become a *philosophy of life*, the explanation for everything that matters. When this happens, we can no longer understand 'science' by simply speaking about what scientists do. We are talking about a philosophical position, which we will turn to examine now.

CHAPTER 3
Science as a philosophy

THE PRACTICAL NATURALISM OF SCIENCE

We have looked at science in practice; at what happens when science is done. There is more to science than this, however. 'Science' is also in some contexts taken to be a general view of the world. It is taken as the explanation for the whole of the universe and life, and the only way in which we can answer profound questions. When science is taken as the repository for all meaning, what is being referred to is not just a method of investigation, but a general philosophy of life which might be called 'naturalism'.

Naturalism is a belief that only natural (as opposed to supernatural or spiritual) laws and forces work in the world. Naturalism takes the physical universe as all that exists, and explains whatever happens within that universe in terms of natural events. Naturalism is also linked with other words such as 'materialism' (the view that there is only matter, not souls, spirits or deities) and 'atheism' (the view that there is no God). Since the

eighteenth century, this view has grown in popularity, so
that it is now the assumed view in most secular institutions and publications. It is sometimes fiercely fought for
with an almost religious fervour, but more often it is
simply taken for granted in public life. (It is worth pointing out that a great many working scientists do not
believe in naturalism, even though it has, for historical
and practical reasons, become the accepted *modus
operandi* of their occupation. We will return to this later.)

The public assumption of naturalism has been
greatly bolstered by twentieth century scientific discoveries. It has grown to be a grandiose view, promising that
once science discovers the most basic principles of the
universe—which (it is assumed) it will do eventually—
then it will have provided us with the ultimate
explanation for everything. The Theory of Everything is
expected to unify all our knowledge, and we will understand the universe.

On a rather more limited basis, science has, in practice, traditionally assumed naturalism as a working
hypothesis 'in the lab'. There is an historical reason for
this, which would make a long story in its own right.
One important factor can be found in the seventeenth
century. In the writings of Francis Bacon, and the early
discussion of the Royal Society, we find an agreement
to leave theology outside the laboratory. In practice,
science was to search into the mechanical causes of
things, to discover how things worked in the world.
Theological disputes were to be left for later. One aspect
of this was religious tolerance; the Royal Society
stated that "As for what belongs to the *Members*

themselves, that are to constitute the *Society*: It is to be noted, that they have freely admitted Men of different Religions, Countries and Professions of Life".[1] Theology was not to be a topic of discussion. The members of the Society, Sprat wrote, "meddle no otherwise with *Divine things*, than onely as the *Power*, and *Wisdom*, and *Goodness* of the *Creator*, is display'd in the admirable order and workmanship of the Creatures".[2]

As this quotation reveals, this was not a basis for atheism. Francis Bacon, and most of the members of the Royal Society, considered themselves devout Christians. Bacon thought of the scientist as 'the servant or interpreter of nature'. In discovering the laws of nature, he must acknowledge that God created those laws, and indeed a better understanding of the universe brought about a better understanding of the glory of God. Nevertheless, any detailed theological discussion was understood not to be the job of working scientists (whatever they may do in their time outside Royal Society meetings). Science had a particular, limited place, and a limited scope of investigation.

Another aspect of this is that the kinds of explanations being looked for were mechanical ones—the mechanisms of how things worked. What precisely that means has changed over time; so now, for instance, scientists will speak of fields and forces, which are rather beyond what we would normally think of as mechanism. The basic point remains, however—that science, as

---

1. Thomas Sprat, *History of the Royal Society*, 1667, p. 63.
2. *Op. cit.* p. 82.

established by the Royal Society, aimed to explain how
things work.

It is only more recently in history that this 'pragmatic
naturalism' has expanded to become an (unjustified)
absolute. For Christian reasons, science began by talking
about natural causes only, for science was just that—a
method for investigating natural causes. In recent years,
however, this has been turned on its head so as to claim
that science therefore proves that natural causes are the
only causes. This is a rather bizarre twist of logic, and
only a little examination will show it to be unreasonable.
Whether or not naturalism is true, it cannot be proved
true by the very activity that pragmatically chooses not
to discuss the alternative. The scientific method (as prac-
tised by the scientific community) will never 'discover'
supernatural causes, since it does not look for them and
by definition cannot accept them. This may or may not
be a useful way to investigate the universe, but on its
current constitution that *is* how science investigates the
universe. A theory that incorporates supernatural inter-
vention is, on current widely- accepted understanding,
not a scientific theory.

MECHANISM AND ORDER

There are important implications that flow from the
practical naturalism of science. One is that there will be
significant questions which fall outside the range of
science. For instance, to even begin a scientific investigation, you have to believe that the world will make
sense—that there are consistent reasons for why things
happen. In simple terms, you have to believe that there is

a mechanism to discover; that there is some basic cause that makes things happen.

So far, this belief has been consistently confirmed. There does seem to be a pervasive order in our world that allows us to find underlying regularities to incredibly diverse phenomena, even phenomena which on the surface seem entirely chaotic. Science, adopting a pragmatically naturalistic philosophy, must assume this order; it cannot explain it. It is a necessary assumption if the practice of science is to proceed at all. Without it, no hypotheses could be asserted about anything beyond the earth (or the limited range of space into which humans have penetrated so far). No basic models for chemistry or physics could be built up, and the criterion of repeatability of experiments would be meaningless. The fact that science has proved so successful on this assumption demonstrates that it is a good assumption. The further we investigate, the more underlying order we find in our universe. In fact, it may be said that the assumption becomes the goal. It is the belief that somewhere behind these diverse phenomena is a basic, understandable set of principles, that keeps scientists constantly searching and investigating.

Although science has repeatedly uncovered underlying regularities to diverse phenomena, what science cannot explain on its own is why this regularity is possible at all. Why is it that our universe is one in which things work in such a regular and predictable manner? Why is it that the more we investigate, the more examples of regularity we find? It is very convenient for us that it is so, as it means that our natural inquisitiveness can be rewarded by finding results for our investigation. However, if we accept nothing more than the universe as a self-existent entity (i.e. naturalism), we can never explain *why* it is so.

This problem is sometimes disguised by speaking of 'laws of nature' as ultimate explanations. However a law of nature does not *explain* the regularities it describes. A general law, along with certain initial conditions, can explain a subsequent event; so 'why does that planet move in that way' can be explained (roughly speaking) by the law of gravity along with the specific conditions about the mass of the planet and the other objects nearby. The law, however, does not tell us *why* gravity always acts in that way.

Order is not ultimately explained by laws of nature. Regardless of how we define them precisely, laws of nature are still descriptions of the fact that the objects or events they govern all behave in the same way. They are extremely useful and enlightening things to have, and to discover that so many areas of our universe are beautifully regular and predictable is deeply satisfying. Nonetheless, what we have is still a description of regularity, not an explanation of why the regularity is there to begin with.

A PHILOSOPHY WITHOUT PURPOSE

Another implication of this decision to make science naturalistic is that science is deliberately not about *purpose*. Science looks at how things work and how they develop. It looks at how different parts of the universe interact and what happens when they do. It explains occurrences in terms of wide-scale regularities, and those in terms of even wider-scale regularities. It does not tell us what any of these things are *for*. It does not tell us why they are there. It can give us a physical explanation for why they behave the way they do, but no purpose for these things.

Indeed, why should it? There is nothing wrong with a method that works well for what it does, and no more. Why should science give us all the answers? Why should it be the way to find to the purpose of something? There is no failure in an enterprise not being able to do what it never set out to do.

It is not uncommon to hear, however, that because science cannot give such answers, our questions about purpose are therefore irrelevant. It is said that since science cannot tell us why life arose, there is therefore no 'why'. It just did. This logic is surprising and somewhat foolish. There *could* be a why; it is just that science does not know how to answer it. This in no way rules out the question. Indeed, one would have to be omniscient to be able to rule out the question. As long as we do not know everything, we cannot simply dismiss a perfectly sensible question—particularly when so many people are interested in the answer, and when other areas of human endeavour claim that they *do* have answers. The answers could be wrong; but they at least demonstrate that the question is not yet proved invalid.

A PHILOSOPHY WITHOUT MORAL VALUES
More generally, science is carried on in a context where there is no longer any agreed upon moral framework in

which to place science. It is sometimes suggested, in fairly simplistic views of science, that 'untrammelled' investigation is the ideal—that moral values are not part of science. However, it should be clear that science never proceeds 'untrammelled' by values; in fact, science needs and uses values all the time. The very decisions about what research to fund, which laboratory to support, which projects are allowed and which are not, are full of 'values'. For instance, a major provider of funds for cancer research has recently refused to support any universities which also receive funds from cigarette companies. Animal rights lobbyists have strongly influenced the way in which laboratory experiments on animals can be conducted. The influence of values extends down to the particular choices of individual scientists. We have seen that on a very basic level scientists need to be able to trust each other and depend upon each other's findings. Scientific research is never entirely 'untrammelled'.

However, while science needs and uses values, there is no scientific standard of values. There is no one moral philosophy that is accepted by science; science is still seen as being something separate from moral philosophy. This means that some very important questions are left unanswered. For example, what *should* we do with what we *can* do? We may know how to do something; how do we know if it is right to do it? There are areas of scientific research which raise serious questions about values. Is investigation into the best kind of nerve gas good? Is it all right to research cloning techniques? Is it good that human embryonic cells can be grown in a laboratory? Is it good that safe medical abortion (safe for the mother, at least) is so easily achieved?

We can see the practical limits of science everyday as we look at the world. The problems that fill the pages of science magazines are not just in establishing the science (although that can be difficult enough) but in working out what is right. If or when it is ever established whether global warming is real, what should we do about it? Ban cheap but environmentally unfriendly technology in developing countries? Put a pollution tax on large companies? Enforce trade sanctions on countries which do not meet pollution controls? We have created a terrible mess already. A future where we know even more about how to manipulate the world without knowing any more about what we should do, is a bleak prospect indeed.

Discussion about the internet has been very revealing for the light it throws on the moral problems of the scientific world. What wonderful new technology, some of the rhetoric goes. It will create a global consciousness. Freedom of speech is a reality, censorship being very difficult, if not impossible. More practically, as a research tool the internet is marvellous, and communication around the globe has become ridiculously easy. The dissemination of information is available on a scale never before known. Education for people in geographically remote areas now has immense possibilities. This technology truly is enormously useful.

Yet more recently, moral dilemmas have come to dominate discussion about the internet. Freedom of speech is not so good when it allows obscene and harassing messages to be sent anonymously. Free access to information has problems when that information is overtly racist, or provides dangerous information such as how to build a bomb. Parents who want the advantages of the internet for themselves complain about the obscene literature now accessible by their children. The ease of email is very annoying when it is used for unsolicited advertising. To some extent, public opinion can regulate what is available; high levels of complaints to a provider can demonstrate that it is in the provider's interest to ban certain customers or pages. To a small extent, legal control of providers has affected the availability of information. However, the problem of how to decide between what is good and what is bad about free information—and worse still, what to do about it—has become frighteningly clear.

Science and technological developments may enable us to live more comfortably, but they cannot show us how to live *well*. Because scientific explanation does not comprehend purpose, it cannot answer very important questions about our world. It may help combat certain types of suffering, but it cannot teach us how to live with suffering. It may explain the genetic similarities between people who act violently, but it cannot explain what is wrong with violence. It may some day even be able to specify the chemical changes in the brain when a person experiences love, but it cannot teach how to love. This is no pious disclaimer; it is something that needs to be taken seriously—*science does not have all the answers.* What it does, it does well. It provides empirically supported information, and produces technology which enables us to manipulate the world. Within its own criteria of success, it is fairly successful. It often provides answers for the questions it poses. However there are other questions.

A thoroughly naturalistic philosophy must face this challenge, as must those who wish to claim that science provides the answers to life and meaning. For not only does science not answer these questions, it also fails to provide the way in which we can make sense of the questions. If there is nothing beyond evolved matter, in what sense can we sustain categories such as 'better' or 'worse'? Not only can science not provide the answer for how to use science for the good, a philosophy that accepts no existence beyond the physical universe cannot explain how we have a category such as 'good' at all. A naturalistic science *must* be limited to an explanation of how things work and no more. If there *is* nothing more than matter changing and reforming itself, on what basis can we have any more? Any notion of 'thought', of 'consciousness', of 'love', of 'personhood'? If the naturalism of science is taken as a whole philosophy, it will not provide a satisfying basis for the reality of these things which we experience every day.

RELIGION CREEPS BACK IN

As we read popular science literature, we find that even those who would want science to be everything do not really act as if they do. Naturalism has won as the dominant ideology of public Western discourse. God has been

banished to the realm of private spirituality, a matter of
opinion and 'faith' (as opposed to 'knowledge'). Yet reli-
giosity will not die, even within science writing which
stays strictly within the bounds of reasonable, publish-
able science (as opposed to the new age speculations
about bizarre properties of physics). Writers of science
can be remarkably religious in the language they use,
and not at all shy about being so. Two examples of
recently published science writers illustrate the point.

Richard Dawkins, as much for his high public profile
as for the tenacity with which he promotes his beliefs, is
a prime example. His book titles deliberately pick up
Christian metaphors to play upon. But while *The Blind
Watchmaker* is a clever pun which replaces the biblical
idea of God with the naturalistic idea of Darwinian
selection, *River out of Eden* takes this one step further.
The river of DNA really does flow, in the bodies of living
creatures through time, from the Eden of our origins.

The appropriation does not stop with the title.
Dawkins writes that the scientific story of evolution does
not just replace the biblical account of creation; it is not
merely science replacing religion, but science becoming
the new religion. It fulfils the function of the old religion,
but more fully, with a greater beauty and depth of
emotion. If Dawkins succeeds in his contrast of science
with the biblical 'myth', we will "find the truth more
interesting, maybe even more poetically moving, than
the myth" (p. 33). Dawkins has also half-jokingly (but
only half) suggested teaching science in religious education classes.

Another science writer of a rather different kind,

Stuart Kauffman, also makes much of religious language. Kauffman is not a popularist in the sense that Dawkins is, expounding and arguing for a well-known and established theory. He argues for a particular theory of origins which is more idiosyncratic than mainstream. Kauffman promotes complexity theory, which uses chaos theory to explain the origins of self-replicating organisms. It is a theory grounded in mathematics, and which Kauffman claims will be undergoing biological testing in the next few years—in other words, he claims that it is well within the realm of experimental science. Nevertheless, Kauffman's book frequently invokes highly emotive and religious language—deliberately so—as part of the search for origins.

We have lost a sense of the sacred, Kauffman claims, and this is one of the essential problems of humankind this century. We are in need of a new creation myth—not just details of what happened in creation, but what it means. It seems it is no longer enough to have knowledge of how something works. In the end, that is rather dull. And thus, the very writers who are most insistent that knowledge of the workings is all we have, demonstrate that to be satisfying, more has to be included in the narrative.

What do we make of this infusion of religious language into scientific writing? Perhaps this is simply a matter of prose—biblical metaphors are rich in meaning, and some very elegant writing can result from borrowing these images. But it is more than that. Much of Dawkin's writing is reminiscent of that other great apologist for naturalistic science, Thomas Huxley. He is not simply pitting science against religion; he is appropriating the language of religion and claiming it for science. Kauffman's approach is somewhat gentler, but still pushes biblical ideas out of the way in favour of a new religion of science.

Perhaps it is not so easy, after all, to be rid of a sense of the sacred. Nature may have been stripped of spirit and deity, but the human soul is harder to domesticate. It seems it is not enough to see the natural world as an intricate clockwork machinery, the unthinking work of a blind watchmaker. Even the most ardent naturalists sense the need for some meaning or poetry to infuse deeper significance into our world.

SCIENCE AND ITS LIMITS

This survey might seem to leave a rather negative impression of science. The emphasis has, indeed, been on what science *cannot* do rather than what it can. In one sense, this has been in response to the recent rise of a genre of popular scientific writing which claims far too much for science. Unfortunately, it is difficult within a short space to provide a completely balanced view of what science is and what it can achieve. However, we should not lose sight of the fact that science has proved an immensely powerful vehicle for discovering what happens in our world, and has undeniably transformed our society—in many ways for the better. Science practice and theory demands a very high level of intellectual endeavour and we find in scientific fields many of the best brains of our society.

As long as science continues to achieve intellectual

success, it deserves some level of recognition. Science provides a very useful method for finding out things about the way the world works. It has become a powerful social force, has transformed Western culture, and had a significant effect on most others. It is one of the greatest testimonies yet to human ingenuity. Perhaps it is because of this very success that some of its most famous popularists have made quite radical claims for it. No longer is science just a technique for discovering mechanical knowledge; it is celebrated as the ultimate source of meaning for life. This conundrum—the naturalistic philosophy which has virtually become a dominant religion—is one of the most peculiar features of modern Western society.

The strength of science, however, must be found in recognizing its valid limits. When proponents of scientific thinking move to being prophets of life and meaning, science is weakened for it cannot sustain such a role. The intellectual machine which seeks to crack the secrets of the physical universe is strongest when it tempers its own pronouncements. It must be added that the vast majority of working scientists *do* temper their own pronouncements; the language of actual scientific papers is generally not in absolutes, but in qualified phrases which keep to the data. It is not the actual publications of science which claim that science is the key to the meaning of everything, but the more popular works. In aiming to make the riches of science available to a wider audience, the claims of science have often been overstated.

This is important to recognize as we now go on to consider the biblical perspective on the natural world.

For in many ways, what the Bible says about the world, and the information we can gain from it, is quite consistent with the scientific endeavour. The Bible has a very positive attitude towards the natural world and towards investigating it. It also recognizes the limitations of such knowledge. It may be surprising that as we turn to look at what the Bible thinks of the world and our knowledge of it, we find some very familiar themes.

Part II
CHRISTIANITY

We started with the aim of understanding how science relates to Christianity, and why there is so often seen to be conflict between the two. We began by looking at science, at what it is and where it came from, and at some of the myths and misunderstandings that have accrued around it.

Now we turn to Christianity, and once again our chief task will be to clarify what Christianity actually is, and what it says about the world. While it might be interesting to trace the history of one Christian view or another, or what different denominations have said, it is the text of the *Bible* which will concern us here. The Bible is the foundational and authoritative document for Christians. It alone is definitive of what Christianity stands for.

One of our problems in doing so is that misunderstandings and misrepresentations of biblical Christianity abound. Most people have very little Bible knowledge, and to make matters worse there are frequently very inaccurate statements (even total misunderstandings) reported in popular literature and the public media. Just as in science, we must not assume that we know what the Bible says before we actually examine it to find out. If we are to understand the relationship between science and Christianity, we need to make sure we are accurately reporting what the Bible says.

Before we begin, however, we might take a few moments to address a couple of common and very basic mistakes that people make even before they approach the Bible.

FAITH VERSUS REASON

"Faith is believing something you know isn't true", might sum up what most people think of faith. Indeed the Oxford Dictionary defines 'faith' (in part) as "spiritual apprehension of divine truth apart from proof". There is a gradation of certainty about knowledge, it seems. Some things are facts, based on reason and evidence. That is knowledge. Other things are without evidence or reasons—and when you have to believe something without evidence, then you need 'faith'.

This kind of understanding of the difference between science and religion is very wide-spread, but it is almost completely wrong. It distorts science, and it is totally inaccurate in its depiction of biblical 'faith'.

In the Bible, 'faith' and 'belief' are mostly interchangeable words; in the New Testament, they are translations of the same group of Greek words. They could also be translated with words such as 'trust', 'depend', or 'rely'. To have faith in something, or to believe it is true, means to trust the evidence and reasons for it. The apostle Paul believed that Jesus rose from the dead. He depended on the fact. He had a personal knowledge that it was true. Why? Because he had a very good reason—he had *seen him*. He had previously trusted (had 'faith') that Jesus was not raised, and had persecuted Christians for their belief in it. But having seen the risen Christ, and heard the testimony of others who had similarly seen him in a variety of circumstances, Paul accepted it as true (cf. 1 Corinthians 15:5-8; Acts 26:25). His *faith* was based on the *reasons* he had for his faith.

The Bible never encourages people to take 'a blind leap in the dark'. On the contrary, it encourages people to use their minds, to think, to find out the truth. The Bible goes into a great deal of detail to give sufficient evidence for the claims that it makes. For instance, the apostle John tells us that he wrote his account of Jesus' life for a specific purpose: "that you may believe that Jesus is the Christ, the Son of God" (John 20:31). No-one was expected simply to believe everything blindly without good reason. Far from it. Luke says of his Gospel that he wrote it "since I myself have carefully investigated everything from the beginning"; and that it was written so that "you may know the certainty of the things you have been taught" (Luke 1:3-4).

To make a distinction between science and Christianity on the basis that one uses reason and the other faith, is to misunderstand both completely. Just as you may have faith (or believe) that the earth moves around the sun because of the reasons and evidence for

it, so you may believe that Jesus lived because of the
reasons and evidence for it. You may also decide that one
of these is wrong; but in both cases, you should study the
evidence before deciding.

WHAT DOES 'LITERALLY' MEAN?

People often ask, 'Do you believe the Bible is true?'.
They then ask a further question: 'But do you believe it
is *literally* true?'. The problem is, it is often unclear what
the difference is between the two questions. The word
'literally' is thrown around a lot, and often used as a criticism: 'If you don't believe it's literally true then you
don't really believe it'. The difficulty is in working out
what 'literally' means; it is often used either ambiguously
or applied inappropriately.

It may be stating the obvious, but the Bible is a book,
or rather a collection of 66 books. It contains poetry,
historical narratives, psalms, drama, laws, prophecies,
letters, proverbs, love songs and other literary forms. In
other words, the Bible is a library of different kinds of
literature, and in order to understand it, we must read it
according to the kind of literature we're dealing with. If
we're reading a part of the Bible which is poetic in form,
we shouldn't read it in the same way as we would an
historical narrative—any more than we would read the
back of a cereal packet in the same way as we would
read a legal contract.

We do not have time here to enter the labyrinths of
literary theory and hermeneutics, but perhaps a brief
example may illustrate the point. Psalm 19 says that
God has set up a tent in the heavens for the sun, who

emerges like a bridegroom from his wedding canopy and runs his course across the sky like a strong athlete—and this expresses the glory and wonder of God's creation. As we read this, we know immediately that the author is not making some kind of mechanistic description of a giant tarpaulin that God has somehow erected in the sky. Nor is he suggesting that the sun has legs. Nor is he making a scientific assertion that the sun moves while the earth stands still. To derive information of that kind from the psalm, or to suggest that the psalmist was even addressing these matters, is to do terrible violence to the psalm as a piece of writing. The author is simply using the very normal techniques of poetry and imagery to make his point, the kind of imagery we use every day when we speak of 'sunrise', even though we now know that the sun does not 'rise' at all, but is stationary in relation to the earth.

What would it mean, then, to read Psalm 19 'literally'? If by 'literally', we mean to read it according to the kind of 'literary' work it is, then we would learn from the author that the daily path of the sun is a grand and majestic thing that expresses God's glory and greatness. Moreover, the poetic picture he draws helps us appreciate what he means; it actually conveys some of that grandeur and strength in a way that a very plain description would not. However, if by 'literally', we mean that the author was really trying to tell us that there was a tent up there, or was arguing for a geocentric universe, we are not just reading the Bible poorly—we are reading poorly full stop. We would not normally read *anything* in that fashion. All reading involves understanding the kind of thing we're reading (the 'genre'), and adjusting our perceptions and reading style accordingly. We do this quite automatically in our daily lives, as we read a newspaper editorial, a cartoon, a letter from a friend or a glossy magazine ad. It seems, however, that people often leave these everyday skills behind when they approach the Bible.

Perhaps it would be better to drop the word 'literally', and simply *read* the Bible, paying due respect to the kind of literature we are dealing with at different points. That is what we will attempt to do in this book.

There are various other misunderstandings about the Bible which will be addressed as we look at what the Bible actually says in relation to the physical world. For we will find that, although the Bible is primarily about God and his relationship with humanity, there is still quite a lot of material about God's relationship with the physical world. We can build a fairly comprehensive biblical picture of how the world runs and what knowledge we can have of it. In fact, this is the very starting point of the Bible.

CHAPTER 4
God and his world

GOD CREATED EVERYTHING

Perhaps the most famous verse in the Bible, with the possible exception of John 3:16, is the first verse of Genesis: "In the beginning God created the heavens and the earth". It is the first and one of the most basic truths of the Bible.

It is important to recognize that the biblical view contains certain important differences from other traditions of divine creation. The most significant is that God created *everything*, even basic matter, out of nothing. He did not just mould or form the universe from pre-existent matter, as Plato held; nor was he the first cause of an eternal universe, as Aristotle taught. In contrast to these views, the Bible makes it quite clear that God brought the universe into being. "Has not my hand made all these things, and so they came into being?" God says in Isaiah 66:2. And as the writer to the Hebrews puts it: "The universe was formed at God's command, so that what is seen was not made out of what was visible" (Hebrews 11:3).

The doctrine of creation implies exactly that—
creation, not crafting. The Bible consistently comes back
to this idea to emphasize God's power and authority over
nature. The universe is his, and he deserves great honour
for having made it and everything in it (Revelation 4:11).

The basic biblical doctrine of creation has further
implications which are important to note—not least
because we have inherited them as part of the Western
intellectual tradition and take them largely for granted.
For example, an important implication of creation is that
the world is *external to God*. The Bible has no room for
a pantheist conception of nature, in which divinity is
contained within the physical world, and in which every
tree and bird and astral body is animated by its god.
However, the biblical doctrine of creation affirms that
although creation is external to God, it is no less *real* for
being so. Physical matter is not illusory or in some sense
a lesser reality, as it is in the Platonic tradition and in
Eastern religion (such as Hinduism or Buddhism). The
creation has a reality and integrity of its own, because
God created it that way. Further to this, as the good
Creator surveys his handiwork, his assessment of the
creation is that it is *very good*—by which he means that
it beautifully fits the purposes he has in mind for it. And
related to the goodness of the creation is its basic ratio-
nality and *order*. The creation account in Genesis 1
emphasizes by its highly ordered, and carefully worked
literary structure, that God created the world as an
orderly and rational place. The world is not chaotic or
haphazard. It is organized and intelligible, because it
owes its existence and shape to the rational creative

word of an all-wise Creator.

We have only touched upon these themes very briefly, and we will return to some of them in due course, but it should be clear that even at this basic level, the Bible's doctrine of creation is not only thoroughly consistent with the scientific endeavour, but provides a conceptual basis for it. It is a little harder to see how a thorough-going animist or platonist or Buddhist could have any motivation or conceptual framework for the practice of what we call 'science'. But for the biblical Christian, the very fabric of God's creation provides a rationale for the scientific enterprise.

GOD UPHOLDS EVERYTHING

Beyond the particular act of creation, however, the Bible constantly refers to an idea that is less well-known, and certainly less well understood. It is rather ironic that one of the most fundamental teachings of the Bible (and one of the most important for the science-religion debate) is so poorly grasped. It is this: that God not only made the world, but he continues to sustain and uphold it.

Simply put, this might not seem so astounding. However, it runs counter to a very common view (with a long history) that sees God as the creator of the machine of the universe, which now continues to run all on its own. Indeed, since the seventeenth century, it has not been uncommon for Christians to praise God for the excellence of his clockwork that it does run so well on its own. Generally speaking such a view is known as deism, in which God is seen as the originator of the universe but distant from it thereafter. God 'wound up' the clock at the beginning, and (in deterministic versions of the view) even determined exactly what would happen from there on; but since then, it runs all by itself, the internal mechanism working away to keep the whole thing ticking.

Even among theists and Bible-believers this idea creeps in. Because 'nature' seems to work so well, and we can perceive physical causes for events, it is easy to think of the world as carrying on by itself. God may well be creator, and even (if we are particularly biblical) may oversee the process, but a latent deism is still very common in everyday discourse.

However, deism (or its atheist cousin 'materialism') is built on the strange assumption that "if something goes on repeating itself it is probably dead" (as G. K. Chesterton so pithily put it). Why should this be the case? Why should the apparent regularity and 'repeatability' of the world signify God's absence? Might it not more reasonably indicate the vitality of his ongoing presence?

The Bible certainly sees it this way. It makes clear that God not only creates the world but continues to uphold it at every instant. Perhaps the word 'create' misleads us here, for when we as humans 'create' something (a work of art, a building, a computer) we sit back and look at it, even walk away and never think of it again, and the object continues to operate. Not so with God, the Bible says. The universe continues to exist every instant because God wills it to. Particles collide and bounce back with conserved momentum because it is God's pleasure that they continue to do so. Galaxies move because God moves them. Every decay of every atom, every combination of molecules with other molecules, every twig that falls off a branch does so because God decides that it will be so.

This may be a fairly challenging idea to the modern mind, and so it is worth seeing in some detail that the Bible really supports this view.

Psalm 104, for instance, speaks of creation as it happened in the past, but also in the present tense. God waters the mountains, it says poetically; the earth is satisfied by the fruit of his work. He makes grass grow for cattle, and plants for man to cultivate. The lions seek their food from God. In fact, all creatures look to him for food, which God provides—not 'nature' or 'natural processes'. Job 39:26-27 expresses the same idea: the hawk takes flight because of God's wisdom, the eagle soars and builds a nest at his command. God determines the number of the stars, Psalm 147:4-9 says, and he knows the stars so intimately he "calls them each by name".

The Bible often describes the weather as specifically controlled by God, not just as a matter of miracle but at any time. God speaks and stirs up a tempest, and stills it again, in Psalm 107. That God covers the sky with clouds and supplies the earth with rain, is a common theme throughout the Bible. He shows his kindness by giving rain and crops for everyone, not just his own people (Acts 14:17). Jesus cites this as the reason for loving one's enemies: "Love your enemies and pray for those who persecute you, that you may be sons of your Father in heaven; for he causes his sun to rise on the evil and the good, and sends rain on the righteous and the unrighteous" (Matthew 5:44-45).

In particular, however, God lets his own people know who is responsible for the conditions they find themselves in. "If you follow my decrees and are careful to obey my commands", God says to Israel, "I will send you rain in its season, and the ground will yield its crops and the trees of the field their fruit". Otherwise, "I will break down your stubborn pride and make the sky above you like iron and the ground beneath you like bronze. Your strength will be spent in vain, because your soil will not yield its crops, nor will the trees of the land yield their fruit" (Leviticus 26:3-4, 19-20; see similar passages in Deuteronomy 28:12, 22). When disaster strikes, God takes direct responsibility: "When anyone came to a heap of twenty measures, there were only ten. When anyone went to a wine vat to draw fifty measures, there were only twenty. I struck all the work of your hands with blight, mildew and hail, yet you did not turn to me" (Haggai 2:16-17; see similar sentiments in Amos 4:9).

This continuous supervision and action by God in the world is the grounds for relying upon God, as Jesus teaches in Matthew 6:25-34.

> Therefore I tell you, do not worry about your life, what you will eat or drink; or about your body, what you will wear. Is not life more important than food, and the body more important than clothes? Look at the birds of the air; they do not sow or reap or store away in barns, and yet your heavenly Father feeds them. Are you not much more valuable than they? Who of you by

worrying can add a single hour to his life?

And why do you worry about clothes? See how the lilies of the field grow. They do not labour or spin. Yet I tell you that not even Solomon in all his splendour was dressed like one of these. If that is how God clothes the grass of the field, which is here today and tomorrow is thrown into the fire, will he not much more clothe you, O you of little faith? So do not worry, saying, 'What shall we eat?' or 'What shall we drink?' or 'What shall we wear?'. For the pagans run after all these things, and your heavenly Father knows that you need them.

Later in Matthew 10:29-30, we have similar teaching: "Are not two sparrows sold for a penny? Yet not one of them will fall to the ground apart from the will of your Father. And even the very hairs of your head are all numbered. So don't be afraid; you are worth more than many sparrows."

Moreover, God does not only provide sustenance for life, he gives life itself to animals and humans. "When you take away their breath", Psalm 104 says of the animals, "they die and return to the dust; when you send your Spirit, they are created". It is the same for people: God not only "spread out the earth" but "gives breath to its people, and life to those who walk on it" (Isaiah 42:5). Although human procreation is a 'natural' process, it is God who "settles the barren woman in her home as a happy mother of children" (Psalm 113:9); it is he who "opens her womb" (Genesis 29:31) and knits the child together *in utero* (Psalm 139:13). God is even in charge of what skills and abilities people develop (Isaiah 54:16-17; Psalm 144:1; Exodus 31:1-6).

All these examples teach in detail what is said in the more general statements such as Hebrews 1:3, "The Son is the radiance of God's glory and the exact representation of his being, sustaining all things by his powerful word" and Colossians 1:17, "He is before all things, and in him all things hold together". The God of the Bible is not a one-off creator. He is not a powerful but distant deity, distributing gifts when he feels like it and doing the odd miracle. He is not even just the overseer of the world. He is the basic power of the world, the reason behind all events, the one who makes things happen, and at whose command the universe continues to exist and hold together. To quote Chesterton again:

> A child kicks his leg rhythmically through excess, not absence of life. Because children have abounding vitality, because they are in spirit fierce and free, therefore they want things repeated and unchanged. They always say, "Do it again"; and the grown-up person does it again until he is nearly dead. For grown-up people are not strong enough to exult in monotony. But perhaps God is strong enough to exult in monotony. It is possible that God says every morning, "Do it again" to the sun; and every evening "Do it again" to the moon.[1]

---

1. G. K. Chesterton, *Orthodoxy*, Fontana Collins, p. 59

GOD WORKS IN DIFFERENT WAYS

Bearing in mind God's continued sustaining and upholding of the world, we can move onto the next idea, which is that God does things in a range of different ways. He uses a variety of means and mechanisms in his constant supervision and sustaining of the world. Let us examine this further.

Order and pattern

We will examine this more fully below, but it is worth mentioning here that God's normal way of acting is through the regular, predictable run of events that we all expect: the turning of the seasons, the sending of wind and rain, of sun, of crops growing and animals living and dying. Most of the time, God does things in this reliable and (to us) predictable way, and because he is trustworthy we expect him to continue to do so.

An illustration may help. If a sparrow stops beating its wings, we expect it to fall to the ground. In fact, the falling of things to the ground happens so regularly and predictably we call it a 'law' and give it a name ('gravity'). However, from the Bible's viewpoint, the 'law of gravity' is simply a description of the regular and predictable way God operates in the world when it comes to things falling to the ground. In fact, no sparrow falls to the ground "apart from the will of your Father" (Matthew 10:29). We may describe it as a regular occurrence of nature, and even plot the sequence of natural causes and effects, but as we do we are only describing the order and pattern which God has built into our world, and which he continues to supervise and uphold moment by moment.

This regular activity of God is quite consistent with what we would expect from his character and purposes. He created the world to be a good and habitable place, not a chaotic and capricious environment. He wanted a place fit for humanity to dwell in and to rule (as we will see in chapter 5). As Isaiah puts it: "For this is what the Lord says—he who created the heavens, he is God; he who fashioned and made the earth, he founded it; he did not create it to be empty, but formed it to be inhabited—he says: 'I am the Lord, and there is no other'" (Isaiah 45:18).

It is also worth noting that sometimes what we call 'normal' or 'natural' events can have a special significance because of their context—the storm that threatened Jonah's ship, for instance, or the quail that were blown towards the Israelite's camp in Numbers 11:31, or the storm that sank Paul's ship. For the God who controls all events in any case, the use of 'normal' occurrences to achieve his purposes is not a problem.

Chance

Humans have traditionally had a concept of 'chance' or 'luck'. This is quite a vague idea, but generally refers to the fact that there are certain events whose outcome we cannot predict, and which seem to us random. Even if we acknowledge that there are causal chains leading to the outcome, we seem to have little or no control over them, or there are too many possible outcomes to predict—and so we think of such events as happening by 'chance'. We even make games out of such events, the thrill of the game being in the very chance nature of them: dice, cards, lotteries. If we want to make a decision based purely on luck, not rational decision, we might toss a coin.

For most of our talk of chance, we still assume that there are physical causes; we just cannot predict them. The number that turns up on the dice was physically determined by the particular force of the muscles in the hand, the friction from the table and so on; we merely call it 'chance' because we do not know the outcome. When people have 'chance' encounters, they both may have arrived at the spot through ordinary means; it is simply the fortuitous crossing of their paths which seems strange. Chance, coincidence and good fortune are all causal; they just seem strange.

The Bible says it is God who decides the outcome; it is he who makes the coin come down on one side rather than the other, or who supervises the 'fortuitous' crossing of paths. They are not in that sense chance events at all. "The lot is cast into the lap, but its every decision is from the Lord", says Proverbs 16:33. It was on this basis that the disciples were confident to choose a successor to Judas in Acts 1. With two candidates who fulfilled the requirements, they simply drew lots to choose who had the job. The fact that the decision was based on 'chance' was not in itself ungodly, for God controls 'chance'.[2]

---

2. We could possibly even extend this to explain God as the cause of quantum events, although the Bible obviously does not do this.

Miracles

At other times God makes things happen in a way that
seems totally out of the ordinary. When Jesus rose from
the dead, that seems totally outside the normal run of
events. God sent manna from heaven for the Israelites in
the desert in a way that appears to be not just strange,
but very hard to explain in terms of the normal working
of the world. A hand appeared out of thin air and wrote
on a wall for Daniel. Many of the miracle accounts show
that God has, at times, done things that were quite
beyond people's expectation of how the world works.

Miracles are often defined as "interrupting the laws
of nature", or some similar phrase. The problem with this
from a biblical point of view is that there are no 'laws of
nature', as such; unless in the sense that nature obeys
what God says. There are discussions about whether the
sun 'standing still' in Joshua 10, or even going 'back-
wards' in 2 Kings 20, are physically possible. Considering
the forces involved, and the disruption of the entire solar
system, how could such a thing *possibly* happen? From
the Bible's point of view, however, the more sensible question is: Why not? The earth only moves in relation to the
sun because God wills it so; and if he wants the earth to
slow down, or do something else that creates the impression of the 'sun standing still', that's up to him. So far as
we know, he has only done this twice in the history of the
world, for which we might be grateful, given how confusing it would be on a regular basis.

It is not wise to dismiss reports of extraordinary,
'nature interrupting' miracles simply because we do not
have access to the mechanics of how God achieved it. An

interesting case in point is the extraordinary death of Herod, briefly recorded in Acts 12:

> On the appointed day Herod, wearing his royal robes, sat on his throne and delivered a public address to the people. They shouted, "This is the voice of a god, not of a man". Immediately, because Herod did not give praise to God, an angel of the Lord struck him down, and he was eaten by worms and died (Acts 12:21-23).

To the modern sceptical reader, this report might appear to be the work of an over-enthusiastic but primitive Christian. Struck down by an angel? Eaten by worms and died? Is this not just superstition?

However, when we consult another ancient report of Herod's death by the Jewish historian Josephus, we find that perhaps our scepticism was premature.

> On the second day of the shows, Agrippa put on a robe made of silver throughout, of quite wonderful weaving, and entered the theatre at break of day. Then the silver shone and glittered wonderfully as the sun's first rays fell on it, and its resplendence inspired a sort of fear and trembling in those who gazed at it. Immediately his flatterers called out from various directions, in language which boded him no good, for they invoked him as a god: "Be gracious to us!" they cried. "Hitherto we have reverenced you as a human being, but henceforth we confess you to be of more than mortal nature." He did not rebuke them, nor did he repudiate their impious flattery...Soon after-

wards he was seized with a severe pain in his
bowels, which quickly increased in intensity...He
was hastily carried into the palace, and...when he
had suffered continuously for five days from the
pain in his belly, he died, in the fifty-fourth year of
his life and the seventh year of his kingship.[3]

Medical experts have attempted to diagnose Herod's
ailment, suggesting that it might have been anything
from arsenic poisoning to the rupture of a hydatid
cyst.[4] God struck Herod down, but this in no sense
precludes a medical description of what killed him.

As we look at miracles as they are actually reported
in the Bible, we realise that defining them as "interrupting the laws of nature" is quite misleading. For some of
the miracles *do* use the normal causal structure of the
world. Herod's death is one example. Another is perhaps
the most famous miracle of the Old Testament—the
parting of the Red Sea. Contrary to popular images,
Moses did not hold out his hand and see the waters part.
What the story actually says in Exodus 14:21 is: "Then
Moses stretched out his hand over the sea, and all that
night the Lord drove the sea back with a strong east
wind and turned it into dry land". It was not even
instantaneous. God can do miracles slowly, if he wishes.
It is a miracle because he did it for a specific reason at
that time, not because it was so very extraordinary.

---

3. Josephus, *Antiquities*, 19.343-50.
4. For details, see F. F. Bruce, *The Book of the Acts*, New
International Commentary on the New Testament, 1988, p. 241-2.

In fact, we have no particular reason to suppose that *any* of the miracles lack a cause we would describe as 'natural'. It may be that God did all of the miracles by using some natural process which is not reported. The miracles in the Bible are there to communicate, and their meaning is generally explained in the text or by context. It would not be surprising if details of *how* it was done were not included.

THE WORLD IS ORGANIZED

We shall now consider in more detail what God's normal way of acting is, for this is particularly relevant to science. It is commonplace for twentieth century Westerners to think of the world as orderly. 'Orderly' is a rather abstract concept, for in everyday life the world often appears anything but orderly. Sometimes it rains, sometimes it's windy, sometimes plants grow and sometimes they die, sometimes people recover from illness and sometimes they don't, sometimes we have drought for years and at other times floods. In what sense, then, do we think that the world is 'orderly'?

The orderliness of the world usually refers to the fundamental structures of order that lie behind everyday experience. That is, despite the apparent fluctuations of day-to-day events, there is a basic pattern to the way the world works. This is the assumption behind the mathematical modelling of the universe in which modern science excels. It is assumed that, for a great many phenomena at least, there will be some mathematical way of describing them, and this is what many physicists and applied mathematicians seek. Whether it is the arc of a thrown ball, or the path of an ocean wave, scientists look for a mathematical equation that will describe the consistent, regular 'orderly' behaviour that things in our world exhibit. The triumph of Chaos theory was that behaviour that appeared random and chaotic—the turbulence of water, or weather patterns—could actually be understood by mathematical principles.

This orderliness is taught in the Bible. As we have already touched upon, the very character of the creation account (in Genesis 1) emphasizes the order and ratio-nality by which God made the world. However, there are two further biblical teachings on which the orderliness of the world is grounded. The world is orderly because of God's *character*—as faithful and consistent—and also because he created the world with a *purpose* in mind. Let us look at these two aspects in turn.

The attributes of faithfulness and consistency are closely linked; they mean that God is not capricious or fickle or prone to act on a whim. While God is free and can do whatever he wants to, it is not in his character to be untrustworthy. What he says he will do, he will do (he is faithful); and his character one day is the same as his character the next (he is consistent). When he proclaims his name to Moses in Exodus 34:5-7, God describes his nature as "abounding in love and faithfulness"; it is part of the being of God to keep his promises.

That God is faithful and consistent emerges from his dealings with Israel in the Old Testament. From the beginning of the Bible, we see God making promises, and (as events unfold) keeping those promises. In fact, the entire Bible could be regarded as a record of the promises God made and how he kept them. From Genesis 3:15 when the first hint of a saviour from sin is given, through the promises to Abraham first articulated in Genesis 12:1, the covenant with David in the Promised Land, and through to the ultimate fulfilment of those promises in Jesus Christ, God has kept all his promises.

God can be trusted. However this alone may not be reason enough to be confident of the basic orderliness of the world. It could be that the faithful God did not particularly care about the world, or humans, to bother making it predictable or comprehensible. This is where the other aspect of biblical teaching becomes important—that God made the world with a purpose. Ultimately this purpose is connected with his beloved Son. "All things have been created by him and for him" as the apostle Paul puts it (Colossians 1:16), and we will delve further into this below. However, for the moment we can note that part of God's overall purpose was to make a world that was *habitable*. Isaiah 45:18 says that God "who fashioned and made the earth...did not create it to be empty, but formed it to be inhabited". This echoes Genesis 1:2, which tells us that originally "the earth was formless and empty", but God shaped it for habitation and filled it with good things. God could have kept it chaotic, but he did not; he wanted it filled and orderly.

We have further examples of this idea in Psalm 104. Things happen according to a certain pattern, and it is a pattern particularly suited to human habitation. "The moon marks off the seasons, and the sun knows when to go down." There is provision of food for animals and humans. The lions seek their food by night, and by day man goes out to work. In simple language we are presented with a picture of a world that is habitable, reli-able, and follows a pattern that enables it to be lived in.

Perhaps the one biblical world which sums up the orderly, rational, purposeful nature of the created world is 'wisdom'. Proverbs puts this song into the mouth of Wisdom:

> I [wisdom] was there when he set the heavens in place, when he marked out the horizon on the face of the deep, when he established the clouds above and fixed securely the fountains of the deep, when he gave the sea its boundary so that the waters would not overstep his command, and when he marked out the foundations of the earth. Then I was the craftsman at his side. I was filled with delight day after day, rejoicing always in his presence, rejoicing in his whole world and delight-ing in mankind. (Proverbs 8:27-31).

God created the world through his own immense knowl-edge and insight. He made it according to 'wisdom' (also see Psalm 104:24; Proverbs 3:19-20; Jeremiah 10:12). Thus to live wisely, in the Bible, is to live in harmony with the created order. Wisdom (as a lifestyle) is possi-ble *because* there is created 'order'. The world is not chaotic; it is a good and orderly place from which it is possible to learn. The 'wisdom' literature in the Bible, such as Proverbs, presents a world which works and which makes sense. We are encouraged to learn from principles based on sensible appreciation of the way cause and effect operates in the world. The creation of the world is wise, and we learn wisdom (in part) by understanding God's world.

For all these reasons, the Bible gives us confidence that the world is comprehensible and predictable. Crops can be planted in the expectation that they will grow and a harvest will be reaped. The seasons will follow one another. The stars will follow a certain course and continue to do so.

This is a world which we might well expect to be able to study and investigate; a world we might come to understand, and therefore to manipulate technologically; a world ripe for 'science'.

If this sounds very promising (and in one sense it is), we must pause to consider a factor which we have so far left to one side: the human factor.

CHAPTER 5

Humanity in God's world

We have seen how the Bible teaches that our world, inhabitable and organised as it is, reflects God's character. It is a predictable world which we might expect to be able to investigate and describe. However, as we have already noted, everyday life often does not seem predictable. Sometimes crops are destroyed by hail, or drought. Sometimes despite the basic pattern of the seasons, there are exceptionally harsh winters or long summers. Things go wrong.

We live in a good world that is nevertheless fallen and distorted. The story of how this situation arose is tied up with the place of humanity in creation, and our relationship to the Creator. This is an issue which we must deal with, if only briefly, before we consider in more detail how we might investigate and study God's world.

HUMANITY IN CREATION

The creation of man and woman is in many respects the pinnacle of God's creative work. In Genesis 1, the consistent pattern of the account suddenly changes after God has made the animals. He now considers how he will make a being who is like himself, and who will have a particular relationship not only with himself, but with the rest of the created order:

> Then God said, "Let us make man in our image, in our likeness, and let them rule over the fish of the sea and the birds of the air, over the live-stock, over all the earth, and over all the creatures that move along the ground".
>
> So God created man in his own image, in the image of God he created him; male and female he created them. God blessed them and said to them, "Be fruitful and increase in number; fill the earth and subdue it. Rule over the fish of the sea and the birds of the air and over every living creature that moves on the ground." (Genesis 1:26-28).

God creates humanity to rule over the rest of the creation. This is what it means for us to be "in God's image". In the ancient world, rulers used to erect images or statues of themselves in different parts of their king-doms as symbols or reminders of who was in charge of the whole kingdom. Humanity is 'God's image' in this sense. We are set up on earth as representative rulers, to have dominion over the earth as God's representatives. We are to rule the earth under God's authority.

This is seen in Genesis 2 as man names the animals and cares for and works the good garden that God has placed him in. The picture in Genesis 2 is of an ideal world, in which man and woman live in harmony with

God, with one another, and with the rest of the created order.

However, the sad story of Genesis 3 is that humanity disobeys God and rejects his authority. Adam and Eve decide to chart their own course and make up their own rules, in defiance of God. The result is that the harmony of Genesis 2 is shattered. Humanity falls out of relationship with God, with each other and with the rest of the creation. The earth itself is cursed because of man's sin, and now produces thorns and thistles. The whole creation is put out of joint because of its rebellion against the Creator.

This has been the briefest of summaries, but it is the essential background for a biblical theme that is crucial for our understanding of Christianity and science: that humanity is privileged to be able to study and understand and master the created order, and yet at another level finds it mysterious and incomprehensible.

The implications of this idea will occupy us for the rest of this chapter and the next.

THE GETTING OF WISDOM

Wisdom in the Old Testament, as we have already noted, meant living in harmony with the good world God had created. The first and basic element of all wisdom, therefore, was a right relationship with the Creator; or as the wisdom literature repeatedly puts it: "The fear of the Lord is the beginning of wisdom" (see Proverbs 9:10; Job 28:28). The first act of the wise person was to submit to the Creator, to listen to his wisdom, to follow his ways.

However, because of the order and wisdom that God has built into the very nature of the creation, knowledge and 'wisdom' about the world can also be found in some measure through observation and learning. The 'wisdom literature' of the Old Testament is not specific moral or legal instruction from God, as (say) the book of Leviticus is; it is not historical narrative, describing God's dealings with his people. It is writing about the world and the people who inhabit it, about things that can be seen in the experience of life, which can be taught to others as part of the education of the godly person.

For example, the book of Proverbs gives instruction about all sorts of practical matters of life and business, as well as moral and personal insight into character and relationships. Much of it is knowledge which could be gained by anyone with a bit of reflection about the world and people within it; indeed, some parts of Proverbs are very similar to sound advice found in ancient Egyptian writings. These are things which can be observed by those prepared to study their world.

Proverbs gives a very positive picture of knowledge in this world. We can have wisdom and life because both are the gifts of God. Certainly, this requires some discipline and learning, but it is possible. We are in a fallen world, and folly and wickedness lie all around. Nevertheless the person who seeks wisdom will find it. Despite the fact that the world is disrupted, we can still see the underlying order, the cause-and-effect nature of the world, and thus learn at least something of how to live.

The book of Proverbs adds another dimension to the idea of wisdom, which is particularly relevant to how we think about science. It tells us that wisdom is not simply a matter of intellectual activity, for it has a moral context. The wise person will not just know a lot, but will also act morally—for to act otherwise is to act contrary to the way the world is meant to be. Immorality is not just being disobedient, it is *foolish*, defying the wise order in which the universe is made. Lying, unfaithfulness, deceit and violence destroy relationships and lead to sadness and ruin; truth and faithfulness on the other hand, are a much wiser path to follow, for they lead to a better life—"The integrity of the upright guides them, but the unfaithful are destroyed by their duplicity" (Proverbs 11:3).

In one sense, then, biblical wisdom puts some boundaries around the search for knowledge. We can know, for instance, that it is wrong and foolish to kill a human being simply for the purpose of dissecting them to discover more about anatomy. It is wrong and foolish to study interpersonal relationships by committing adultery. It is wrong and foolish to steal results. Obeying God's moral laws is not separate from wisdom; it is part of what the wise person will see as being the wisest thing to do. This was the advice Moses gave the people of God when they were about to enter the Promised Land:

> See, I have taught you decrees and laws as the Lord my God commanded me, so that you may follow them in the land you are entering to take possession of it. Observe them carefully, for this will show your wisdom and understanding to the nations, who will hear about all these decrees and

say, "Surely this great nation is a wise and understanding people" (Deuteronomy 4:5-6).

What kind of learning, then, does the wise person have? What is the intellectual content of wisdom? We might answer this by looking at the great hero of wisdom in the Old Testament, King Solomon.

The most famous stories of Solomon's wisdom are probably those about him ruling and making civil judgements wisely—such as the famous story of the disputed child in 1 Kings 3. However, his wisdom was not simply a matter of affairs of state and justice. It also included literary activity, speaking proverbs, writing songs, and studying nature. It included some of the things we think of as science: he "described plant life, from the cedar of Lebanon to the hyssop that grows out of walls" and also "taught about animals and birds, reptiles and fish" (1 Kings 4:33). 1 Kings 4:1-34 shows the considerable benefits Solomon enjoyed from ruling wisely: administrative power; a great number of prosperous people; tribute from other countries; much material wealth; financial independence for his people; as well as great understanding and insight and enjoyment of intellectual activity. People from all nations came to listen to him; they presumably did not share his knowledge of God, as they were not recipients of the word of God. However his greater insight into knowledge through his God-given gift of wisdom enabled him to instruct others.

The example of Solomon sums up much of the Bible's attitude to what we think of as science, in two very important ways. Firstly, it demonstrates that God's world is good and it is worth studying. However, it also demonstrates that knowledge of the world, when separated from true understanding of its Creator, is disastrous. Solomon, as readers of the Bible know well, did not continue in wisdom. He ultimately turned his back on God—a theological failure which led to his own moral failure and the downfall of his political kingdom. He ceased to fear the Lord, and so in the end ceased to be wise.

Solomon embodies both the power and limitations of wisdom, and indeed of science. He represents the pinnacle of Israel's wisdom, and yet the essence of Israel's failure. He understood much from his study of the world, and was greatly blessed by God, and yet in not obeying God, he ultimately failed to live well in the world. Ultimately, all wisdom (and all science) cannot escape the moral context.

There is another (related) thing which both wisdom and science cannot escape. Despite all we can know and understand about our world, there are boundaries or limits to what we can discover.

CHAPTER 6
The limits of wisdom

The Bible recognises that there is a great deal which can and should be learned from investigating our world. It is not a Christian attitude to try to escape the world in inner contemplation or meditation, or to regard the material world as evil. It is God's creation, and he described it as 'very good'. He created it for our habitation and expects us to learn about and make use of the things he has given us in his wisdom.

However the Bible recognizes what we have already seen in our study of science—that there are limits to what we can learn in this world. There are some things beyond our knowledge and beyond our ability to know. The Bible emphasises that we ourselves are limited, finite beings and we do not have the power of God. Moreover, both ourselves and our world have been corrupted by our own rebellion against God. We can learn a lot from searching the world with the power of our own intellect, but there are still things we do not and will not know through our own talents and endeavours.

THE WORLD IS CONFUSING

Even when we think we know how some things work, we can fall into the trap of believing we know everything. The book of Job is one long challenge to such a simplistic view of the world. Job was a righteous man; he did not understand why his world fell apart. Job did everything right, but it turned out all wrong. His comforters each had various ways of resolving this problem, based on their own simplistic understandings of how the world was. However, none of them worked. Their frameworks of how the world must behave had to be readjusted in light of how the world actually was. The point of the book is that we, the readers, know the metaphysical background to Job's sufferings, but Job and his friends, faced only with the brute physical fact of his suffering, cannot make sense of it. The generalisations of Proverbs, suitable as they are for a large part of life, do not always fit the specifics of experience. Orderliness is not our only experience of the world. We also experience chaos, sudden inexplicable tragedy, and death; in a word, disorder.

That is, we know the order of the universe because we have been told of it, and investigating, we see it. Like Job's comforters, however, we can be tempted to set up rigid laws of nature based on the order we observe, and insist that nothing else can happen. However, what we generally observe does not constrain God, and he may do things beyond our understanding. We don't know why one particular individual is suffering more than another. There are some answers we cannot work out from our own investigation. The book of Job reminds us that in the end, just as we trust the world to be orderly because God has made it so, so we must trust God to continue ruling in his wise and just way. Either way, we do not have ultimate power over God or the universe; we have the delegated power he has given to us.

The book of Ecclesiastes also demonstrates the limits of wisdom. The order within the universe is mysterious; and because of our sin, it is confused, and so are we. Ecclesiastes expresses the confusion we feel when the world looks as if it ought to make sense, but refuses to be made sense of. "I devoted myself to study and to explore by wisdom all that is done under heaven", the writer tells us at the start. "What a heavy burden God has laid on men! I have seen all the things that are done under the sun; all of them are meaningless, a chasing after the wind" (Ecclesiastes 1:13-14). Although his wisdom gave him greater insight, the insight did not satisfy him, for the more he knew, the more confused he became.

> I thought to myself, "Look, I have grown and increased in wisdom more than anyone who has ruled over Jerusalem before me; I have experienced much of wisdom and knowledge". Then I applied myself to the understanding of wisdom, and also of madness and folly, but I learned that this, too, is a chasing after the wind. For with much wisdom comes much sorrow; the more knowledge, the more grief (Ecclesiastes 1:16-18).

It is a confusing world described in the book of Ecclesiastes. It is, in fact, the world we live in, pictured with shattering clarity. We see the existence of good and bad, of joy and sorrow, but we do not know what that means for our actions—should we live it up and enjoy life, or work hard, or not? We all die in the end, so what is worth doing? It seems somehow intuitively right that wisdom must be better than folly, knowledge better than ignorance, but what does it gain us?

> Then I turned my thoughts to consider wisdom, and also madness and folly. What more can the king's successor do than what has already been done? I saw that wisdom is better than folly, just as light is better than darkness. The wise man has eyes in his head, while the fool walks in the darkness; but I came to realise that the same fate overtakes them both.
> Then I thought in my heart,
> "The fate of the fool will overtake me also. What then do I gain by being wise?" I said in my heart, "This too is meaningless". For the wise man, like the fool, will not be long remembered; in days to come both will be forgotten. Like the fool, the wise man too must die! So I hated life, because the work that is done under the sun was grievous to me. All of it is meaningless, a chasing after the wind (Ecclesiastes 2:12-17).

Even in this world, wisdom will not necessarily receive its reward. This frighteningly apt little story could be read with wry amusement by all manner of intellectuals down the ages:

I also saw under the sun this example of wisdom that greatly impressed me: There was once a small city with only a few people in it. And a powerful king came against it, surrounded it and built huge siegeworks against it. Now there lived in that city a man poor but wise, and he saved the city by his wisdom. But nobody remembered that poor man. So I said, "Wisdom is better than strength". But the poor man's wisdom is despised, and his words are no longer heeded (Ecclesiastes 9:13-18).

While living in this world, wisdom is a good thing; but wisdom has its limits. For one thing, wise or foolish, we all go to the grave in the end. The words of the wise are not remembered and the strong triumph. Great knowledge does not necessarily bring recognition or honour, even when much deserved. In the mass of public opinion, in the fights of the political sphere and power struggles, wisdom is often the last thing to receive its due recognition. Its ideas might be taken advantage of and used to the profit of the powerful, but the person who came up with the idea can forget about receiving credit for it.

In the end, all the knowledge in the world will not save us from death. The wise and the foolish, the intensely knowledgeable and the totally ignorant, all end up in the ground. What, then, is the point of learning?

Wisdom, then, is recognized as having very practical bounds. For all the good it can do, its good is strictly limited. On a more abstract level, however, wisdom is even theoretically limited. There are things in the world that no amount of wise investigation will help us understand. This is the most profound limit of wisdom, and it is recognized by the Bible's wisdom writers. The world is investigable, and a good deal of knowledge can be gained from it, but there comes a point where it all just becomes incomprehensible. Things happen, and we do not know why. Things even happen in an orderly, structured, and seemingly meaningful way, but the meaning escapes us. The world looks so very organized, as if it must have a purpose, but what is the purpose? *What is it here for?* That, not even the investigations of wisdom can tell us.

> When I applied my mind to know wisdom and to observe man's labour on earth—his eyes not seeing sleep day or night—then I saw all that God has done. No one can comprehend what goes on under the sun. Despite all his efforts to search it out, man cannot discover its meaning. Even if a wise man claims he knows, he cannot really comprehend it (Ecclesiastes 8:16-17).

The difference between this and the nihilistic meaninglessness of this century is that the writer of Ecclesiastes never doubts for a moment that God is acting, even if sometimes his actions are beyond us. This is "the burden" God has set upon us: "he has made everything beautiful in its time. He has also set eternity in the hearts of men; yet they cannot fathom what God has done from beginning to end" (Ecclesiastes 3:10-11). Without God's explanation about what he is doing, the seeming purposefulness of the world ultimately remains a frustrating mystery.

The warning of Ecclesiastes is not to depend too much on what we can observe for ourselves in the world. Because it is a created world, and created by a rational and orderly being, we can build up a very comprehensive world-picture, and one that works. However, it is tempting to become over-confident in this world picture, and believe that it makes sense on its own. However, under deeper examination it does not make sense on its own. Ecclesiastes warns us that the cause-and-effect world is not a self-sufficient system. There are still profound questions that remain unanswered, for which we will not find answers within the system itself. There are things that still do not make sense, no matter how much we examine and think about them. We do not see the whole, and do not understand its purpose. The world is the ongoing work of a God who is external to the creation, and who alone understands the whole.

GOD'S REAL POWER

"Our God is in heaven", proclaims Psalm 115, "he does whatever pleases him".

This idea, it has to be said, does not sit well with what we humans like to think. Nevertheless, if we are to understand the relationship between God, us and his world, we must take this view seriously. God is not constrained by our ideas. What he tells us he will do, he will do, for he is faithful; but we cannot assume that he will abide by what *we think* he should do in the absence of such prior information. In his generosity, he has told us a great deal about his work and his plans for the world, but there are many details he has not seen fit to disclose.

Job's friends had some trouble coming to terms with this idea, and Job makes the point rather starkly:

Though one wished to dispute with [God], he could not answer him one time out of a thousand. His wisdom is profound, his power is vast. Who has resisted him and come out unscathed? He moves mountains without their knowing it and overturns them in his anger. He shakes the earth from its place and makes its pillars tremble. He speaks to the sun and it does not shine; he seals off the light of the stars. He alone stretches out the heavens and treads on the waves of the sea. He is the Maker of the Bear and Orion, the Pleiades and the constellations of the south. He performs wonders that cannot be fathomed, miracles that cannot be counted. When he passes me, I cannot see him; when he goes by, I cannot perceive him (Job 9:1-10).

Indeed, the last few chapters of Job make good reading along these lines, and are bound to humble any arrogance. "Where were you when I laid the earth's foundation?" God pointedly asks the embarrassed Job. "Have you ever given orders to the morning, or shown the dawn its place, that it might take the earth by the edges and shake the wicked out of it? Have the gates of death been shown to you? Have you comprehended the vast expanses of the earth?" Furthermore, God points out that he has a certain unchallengeable priority over humanity: "Who endowed the heart with wisdom or gave understanding to the mind?" (Job 38:4, 12-13, 17, 18, 36). We cannot challenge God when it comes to knowledge. Not only do we simply not know as much as he does, nor have the ability to know as much, but any knowledge we do have is there because God gave our minds the understanding.

The book of Job is also pertinent in that it challenges the ability of human technology—powerful though it is—to discover the extent of God's wisdom. We can mine the depths of the land, extract gold and gems, and accomplish more than any other animal. Man "tunnels through the rock; his eyes see all its treasures. He searches the sources of the rivers and brings hidden things to light" (Job 28:10-11). We can discover deeply hidden secrets about the world. "But where does wisdom come from? Where does understanding dwell?" (Job 28:20). It cannot be discovered in the depths of the sea, or bought with all the gold and riches we are able to extract. "God alone understands the way to it and he alone knows where it dwells, for he views the ends of the earth and sees everything under the heavens" (Job 28:23-24).

What the Bible says about our knowledge of God's work in the world goes even further than this. There are some things about God that we will not ever be able to work out. What we know of his plans and his actions, and of God himself, is what he chooses to tell us, not what we can discover on our own. It is a sign of human arrogance that we keep trying—but as God points out in Isaiah 29 (also quoted in 1 Corinthians 1), "the wisdom of the wise will perish". Just as worship that is made up of rules invented by humans will not sway God, reason based on the limited information available to human knowledge will not discern the plans of God. We will only know what he chooses to reveal.

This is not an isolated theme in the Bible. Although it is not often recognized, the Bible is quite clear that there are some things which we can only know by revelation. Knowledge about God and what he does is *revealed* knowledge, not knowledge that is arrived at by empirical investigation.

The upshot of this is that it is worth approaching conclusions about God with some humility. There is a great deal about his work that we cannot know, and cannot work out in advance. While most of the Bible references to this idea concern God's plans for salvation history, it is a worthy principle to remember for any of God's work. *A priori* conclusions about God have little place in the biblical scheme; what we know for sure is what he has told us, and beyond that we should tread very warily. As the prophet Isaiah warns:

> Who has measured the waters in the hollow of his hand, or with the breadth of his hand marked off the heavens?
>
> Who has held the dust of the earth in a basket, or weighed the mountains on the scales and the hills in a balance?
>
> Who has understood the mind of the Lord, or instructed him as his counsellor?
>
> Whom did the Lord consult to enlighten him, and who taught him the right way?
>
> Who was it that taught him knowledge or showed him the path of understanding? (Isaiah 40:12-14).

CHAPTER 7

Wisdom incarnate

We closed our last chapter on a note of mystery, emphasizing that there is still much that we cannot find out by our investigation of the world. There are limits to empirical wisdom. There are some things—like the meaning and purpose of the whole—which elude us, no matter how hard we search. This was certainly the perspective of Ecclesiastes, with its assertion that for all our wisdom and knowledge, we cannot fathom the real mysteries of the universe.

However, this is not the Bible's last word on the subject. The Bible, after all, is an unfolding story, not a collection of sayings or abstract religious truths. It is a drama, a great narrative, in which God's plans progress towards their completion over time. It is a tale of promise and fulfilment.

In Jesus Christ, the Bible emphatically declares, the great secret *has* been revealed. The mystery of God's purposes for the world are finally made known. In God's good time, he has kept his promises by sending his Son into the world to become a man, to be wisdom incarnate.

There are many places in the New Testament which summarize how Jesus fulfils God's plans. The first chapter of Paul's letter to the Colossians explains that in Christ, God answered the dilemma of the fallen, distorted creation. The Son came into the world as the "image of the invisible God", the one who rules the earth as man was created to (vv.15-16). He is the fulfilment of all that Genesis 1 looked forward to. However, he is not only the epitome of Genesis 1; he is the answer to Genesis 3. Jesus reconciled the fallen, rebellious creation to its Creator (vv.19-22). He did this by a strange method, which no-one anticipated (although there were plenty of hints in the Old Testament). In a stunning twist to the unfolding story, the ultimate ruler died on the cross, to pay for and answer the sin and distortion of the world.

By doing so, he opened a path of reconciliation between God and humanity. Now all mankind, both Jew and Gentile, can be part of God's kingdom. God has created a new humanity, a new people who, rather than being estranged from him, now trust him and obey him. In this new people of God, the Son himself is first and pre-eminent and supreme (Colossians 1:18-20).

These are grand, mind-stretching ideas, and they are reflected throughout the New Testament (also see Ephesians 1:1-14; John 1:1-18; Hebrews 1:1-4). The implications are enormous. What we could not determine or discover from looking at the world, God has now revealed through Jesus Christ; namely, what it was all *for*. All the orderliness we perceive in the universe in fact has a purpose: it is for Christ. God always had a plan in creation, and it was that eventually all things would be ruled by his Son, the ultimate image of God, in a perfectly harmonious order. Along the way this plan involved disruption, and for a long time people did not know what it was all heading towards, but now that knowledge has been revealed. As Colossians goes on to put it, Christ is "the mystery of God, in whom are hidden all the treasures of wisdom and knowledge" (Colossians 2:2-3).

Through Christ, God has also revealed the *future*. The distortion and corruption of the current created order will not last forever. What God has done through his Son will one day result in the renovation of all things. The apostle Paul puts it this way:

> I consider that our present sufferings are not worth comparing with the glory that will be revealed in us. The creation waits in eager expectation for the sons of God to be revealed. For the creation was subjected to frustration, not by its own choice, but by the will of the one who subjected it, in hope that the creation itself will be liberated from its bondage to decay and brought into the glorious freedom of the children of God.
>
> We know that the whole creation has been groaning as in the pains of childbirth right up to the present time. Not only so, but we ourselves, who have the firstfruits of the Spirit, groan inwardly as we wait eagerly for our adoption as sons, the redemption of our bodies (Romans 8:18-23).

God's plan will eventually result in an entirely new order of things in which the creation will be "liberated from its bondage to decay". In the meantime, we must endure the suffering that still forms part of the fallen world.

If this is all beginning to sound rather ultimate, and a long way removed from science, it is in fact the framework which makes proper sense of science—for it makes sense of the world which science seeks to investigate. While there is not space to explore them fully here, it can be seen that there are certain conclusions that flow from the knowledge that the purpose of the universe is found in Christ.

For one thing, if we have been reconciled to God through Christ, we are now in an ideal position to understand and investigate the order that is in our world. We are now able to rule the world more success-fully, in a sense, because we are connected to Christ, who is the perfect image of God, the ultimate ruler. We now have a framework for understanding the world as a whole, for we understand what it is for and where it is going. This may not affect the mechanics of how we gather data (apart from informing our ethics), but it will provide a conceptual basis for interpreting and devising theories. It may not mean that Christians will make better scientists—for there are many things that go into making a good scientist—but it does mean that Christians will have a coherent framework for making sense of scientific discoveries, and their application to life in the world.

We can also now understand why humans seem to have such an important place in the world—why it is that we alone have the urge and the ability to investigate the world and make sense of it. Without knowing the ultimate destiny of humanity as revealed in Christ, the privileged position of humanity is hard to make sense of. Indeed, in a completely atheistic world view, it makes no sense at all. Why is it that humans alone have consciousness, language, civilisation, literature—in fact, dominion —especially when we seem similar to other animals in some ways? It does all make sense once we understand that Christ is the first of a new people of God, and that our destiny and value as humans is connected with God's ultimate purposes for the universe.

Much the same is true of the world as a whole. With an understanding of the big picture of God's purposes in Christ, we can make sense of our world, with its strange mixture of goodness and regularity, suffering and chaos. We can know that the world is orderly, and yet that it also suffers from distortion. We can know that humanity's role is to master the world, to care for it, to work it, to supervise it under God's authority. We can also know that there is a certain provisionality about the world as it currently is—that the world is waiting for transformation in God's good time. This will prevent us from falling into the kind of utopianism that sometimes accompanies science—as if by science and technology we will solve all the world's problems and usher in a golden age.

Christ is the key which unlocks the mysteries of our experience. Those things which a purely naturalistic science cannot explain, are now made clear. From the perspective of Christ, we can begin to understand the world as it is, as we experience it—our sense of personhood, of values, of purpose. Everything we do *makes sense* when put in this context.

CHAPTER 8
God and science

We have by now a general picture of what the Bible says about the world—about its creation, its ongoing existence by God's power, its orderly and investigable character, and yet also the confusing and mysterious face it presents to us. We have seen how humanity is privileged to rule the world under God, and is able to investigate, understand and master the world through the faculties God has given us. And yet we have noted too that there are limits to what human wisdom (or science) can discover. Finally, we have traced the biblical story through to its fulfilment in Christ, who alone is the solution to the mysteries of life, and who provides us the key to understanding God's ultimate purposes for us and for the world.

Having sketched the biblical worldview, at least in broad brushstrokes, we can now consider the relationship of Christianity to science. Are the two compatible?

THE PHYSICAL WORLD IS GOD'S WORLD

The physical world was created by God and everything in it continues to be sustained by his will. Thus, any true theory of how that physical world works cannot conflict with a Christian view of God, for the Bible says that the physical world is entirely moved and controlled by God, working in and through what we regard as 'natural processes'.

Important implications flow from this. Firstly, finding a 'natural' cause for an event is no reason to dismiss God as the fundamental cause. In fact, if nothing else, our survey of biblical teaching should make clear that the word 'natural' is rather inappropriate, especially if it is contrasted to 'supernatural'. In the end, there is no difference between the two, in the Bible's view. All causes within the world are ultimately caused by God. So even the most complete scientific theory, with every causal chain thoroughly described, is no reason to conclude that God is not there. From the Bible's viewpoint, it is merely an elaborate description of the wise order that God has created, and now sustains, in the world. The two are not competing explanations; they are both true explanations.

Perhaps this needs to be put in a different way. That is, God was never an explanatory principle whose prime value was in making sense of a confusing world. The Bible never presents that as a good reason for believing in God. In fact, the opposite is the case—that God is there is a good reason for attempting to make sense of the world. Science does not, and cannot, dismiss the need for God, for God is not a competing theory. The Bible does not present God as the explanation for the world which might later be surpassed by a better, scientific explanation; rather, it presents God as the rational Creator of an ordered world, who makes explanation in physical terms possible at all.

Flowing from this we see that finding a 'natural' explanation for miracles does not 'disprove' the miracle. It is ironic that when physical explanations for things such as biblical miracles are found, this is taken as evidence that the Bible is *not* true, or that God did *not* do it. For instance, certain conditions in the Middle East have been discovered under which a wind might significantly lower part of the Red Sea. But this cannot be taken as evidence that it was a purely 'natural' event rather than a miracle—especially since the Bible specifically records the natural circumstances of the event (the 'strong east wind') as part of its description of God's mighty action (see Exodus 14:21-22)

Similarly, there is evidence of a supernova that would have been seen on earth around the time of Jesus' birth. We don't know whether or not this was actually the star mentioned in Matthew which guided the wise men—but even if there was a supernova, this does not reduce the extraordinary and amazing conjunction of circumstances that leads us to call it a 'miracle'. The point is that the finding of physical evidence for a miracle recorded in the Bible is neither here nor there; for God may well have used a normal physical process to bring about his miracle. What is 'miraculous' is the extraordinary nature or significance of the event.

Similarly, events which seem to us a matter of chance are no reason to dismiss God as cause. There are certain events in the Bible which, without explanation, would seem entirely haphazard and coincidental; yet that is nothing to God, who works out his purposes regardless of outward appearances. The fact that we cannot predict the outcome, or that to us certain events seem to be a matter of pure chance and coincidence, says nothing about whether God was involved.

Finally, the fact that God's action in the world is so general and so varied means that we have no way of predicting particular ways in which God will act in nature. We know that we can trust him to be generally consistent, and so we can trust our normal procedures of investigation into nature; but God is not to be constrained by our ideas. He may accomplish his purposes one way, or he may do it another. The Bible provides examples of a range of different ways in which he makes nature behave.

In fact, it is this idea—that God is free to act however he wants to—which gave some impetus to scientific investigation historically. One strand of seventeenth-century thought emphasized that we cannot deduce from first principles how God will behave, for God does what he wants to do. The only way to discover how he has made the world, then, is to investigate it empirically. Our ignorance is what makes scientific investigation so exciting. There could be anything out there: we can only look and see. We have not yet exhausted the wonders of God's creativity.

All of this is to say that whatever kind of religion might conflict with science, biblical Christianity does not. Despite the claims that some make to the contrary, the Bible actually encourages and stimulates science as not merely a possible, but a useful and worthwhile pursuit. The Bible presents a picture of the world as understandable *because* it is contingent upon God, who created it for human habitation and who can be trusted to create and sustain it reliably. The Bible also encourages us to learn from creation—to learn the principles of cause and effect, to consider how to live well, and even specifically to study the details of the created world.

GOD AND TESTABILITY

Some people do not like the notion that God is behind everything, for this means that God cannot be disproved by science, and so the idea is rejected as untestable and therefore meaningless. The problem with this procedure is that it has still not understood what the Bible is saying about God's action in the world. It still rests on the latent deism that wants to see evidence for the supernatural as different from evidence for the natural. It has failed to grasp the radical nature of what the Bible says about God.

As has been stressed several times, God is not an alternate explanation for events. He is not the theory we hold *in contrast* to natural or mechanistic theories. It is not that some things cannot be explained by mechanism and so we turn to a supernatural explanation. The Bible never speaks of God in those terms. Rather, we know that God is behind everything, and we know it because this knowledge has been revealed. We have been told that the universe is God's creation and that he continues to uphold it. We have been told that the purpose of the universe is found in Christ. Having been told that, we are expected to respond in certain ways. This is not our theory to explain the world; it is information we have received from 'outside'. It is the reference point that makes sense of the world.

This is something that God chooses to let us know, not something we have worked out for ourselves. Even at the most basic level, what has been created shows God's eternal power and divine nature, Romans 1 says, but not because we work out God as an explanation of the world, but because God shows his character through what has been made. It is a very important distinction. What we know of God, he has revealed.

That means that God is not testable through 'nature'. The objection is quite right; there is nothing in nature that would disprove God. He is the explanation for everything, and whatever happens, we can say with confidence that God was behind it. We are given no grounds for predicting what God might do and then testing to see whether it happens; God does all sorts of things, and we cannot constrain him in advance to certain activities.

Is Christianity as a religion, then, untestable? In one sense, the question betrays a very narrow and ultimately untenable view of knowledge. The idea that something has to be 'testable' in a strictly empirical sense in order to be known as true is very limited. Indeed, the very idea that all theories have to be testable is itself not a testable assertion, and is therefore proved to be a meaningless theory by its own criteria.

The reasons that go into justifying a belief—any belief—are far more complex than a simplistic view of testability. How does one 'test' the belief that your spouse loves you, for example? There would be a mass of complex interlocking reasons that would lead you to conclude (quite reasonably) that the proposition is true, but it is not something that can be determined in a laboratory by experiment. Belief in the truth of a whole philosophy of life (such as Christianity) has to do with such an interlocking complex of ideas.

However, the question can still be considered on a basic level, if for no better reason than that 'untestability' is still used, unreasonably, as an opposition to Christianity. It is unfortunate that for so long people concerned with 'evidence' for God have tended to look for the 'testability' and 'evidence' in the wrong places; that is, in creation. For the Bible itself points out that the place where Christianity stands or falls, and is 'testable' in our modern language, is not in creation but in the history of Israel culminating in the person of Jesus Christ. If he never existed as a human being, then Christianity is worthless. If he never died, as the Koran says, then the Bible is false and Christians are deluded. If he never rose again, as many Jews believe, then our faith is useless, as 1 Corinthians 15:14 says. If he were not God, or not the Messiah, then Christianity is false. This is why the New Testament books after the Gospels keep pointing back to the events of the Gospels as being of primary importance. If these events did not happen, then no amount of Christian teaching is worth anything.

The life and death of Jesus is a crucially important event to investigate. Not only has it changed the course of human history, the Bible claims it is the central event in eternal history. The truth of Christianity, and (if it is true) the fate of the universe, hang on this one event.

Towards a Christian view of science

We have seen that much of the supposed conflict
between science and Christianity is actually not found in
the Bible. Not only does the Bible encourage us to study
the world, but it recognizes the sensible limitations of
such study—as indeed good science does. More than
that, however, the Bible can provide the further answers
that we do not find from studying the world—that is,
what it is for, what it all means, and how we should live.
So far, we have found no real conflict between believing
the Bible and undertaking science.

We will now pull together some of these ideas, as we
construct the beginnings of a Christian view of science.
If it is not conflict, what is it?

Science in practice

First of all, let us consider science as an activity, as
described in Part I. It should be clear by now that the
Bible is in favour of investigating the world. It is God's
world, after all, and it is only appropriate that as care-
takers of his world we should be interested in how it
works. Anyone who takes the Bible seriously has excellent motivation to take up science, if he or she so wishes.

What is more, we have a motivation to take up
science through the empirical method. While there is not
space here to go into the philosophical complexities—or
the historical background—the biblical understanding
would lead us to think that empiricism is an appropriate
method for investigating the world. That is, the Bible
shows us that God acts in the world the way he wants
to. He has not given first principles from which we can

deduce logically how the world *must* be. The only way we can discover how the world is, is to look at it. The only way to find out how it works, is to investigate. If we are interested in how the world is put together in a functional sense, we do not simply ponder in our heads, or wait for revelation from God—we go and use our senses and our brains to find out.

Moreover, again in a basic sense, the Bible gives us some confidence that we will be able to make discoveries, and accumulate a body of knowledge. Along the way we are bound to make mistakes, and we will always be limited in what we know, for we are finite beings. However we can be hopeful that the empirical method will give us the information we want—and with more reason than simply that it has seemed to work well enough so far. We have a justification from outside the system that our hope for knowledge is not in vain. The God who made us also made the world for us to inhabit, to rule and use wisely. The world is not an amalgam of chance events—it was something created deliberately, with humans given a special place in it. From the Bible's point of view, it is not at all surprising that our scientific efforts have enjoyed the success that they have.

When we look at science as a community of people, too, we see a concordance with Christian principles. The scientific community expects and requires truthfulness from its scientists; a quality that Christians uphold in any sphere. The cooperation and teamwork of science assumes principles of relationship which are in harmony with Christian thinking, Christianity being fundamentally about relationships. The things which mar good science, and make the working scientists' life more difficult—competitiveness, the pressure to publish, the scrambling for funds, the fights over prestige and precedence—are the outworkings of selfish human nature. Christianity provides a motivation and basis for the kind of behaviour which make the scientific community work. An atheistic pragmatism can only recognize the value for the community of good behaviour; it does not provide motivation for the individual to practise it.

Science as philosophy

This leads us to the broader issues concerning science. Far from being in conflict with science, Christianity actually provides a theoretical underpinning for science which naturalism cannot. As we have seen, science pragmatically limits itself to being naturalistic, to not discuss things like morality and purpose. However science needs a framework of morality and purpose to work at all. They are necessary concepts that underlie scientific method, although scientific method itself does not provide them.

For instance, we have seen that a basic assumption of science is that the world is ordered. Science within a Christian framework has a reason for this assumption; within a naturalistic framework it does not. We have also seen that the Bible provides the idea of purpose which naturalism excludes. We need not be limited to the mere understanding of mechanism. We need not be baffled by the astounding fact that humans have such complex minds. We need not be astonished by the inexplicable wonder of the universe's being here at all. We can see that it does all fit together, there is a reason. Our sense of meaning and purpose is real. We can see that the world is not just a matter of heartless, pitiless, valueless molecules—that rather we and our thoughts and feelings and moral impulses *matter*.

Understanding the Bible also provides the moral framework which science needs, but which naturalism cannot provide. The Bible shows that learning and investigating are not value-free. There are ways of investigating that are wrong. The Bible can give reasons for the moral indignation that people feel against cruel animal experimentation, or Nazi experimentation on humans. A biblical view of science shows that learning wisdom from the world includes obeying God's moral law, and that knowledge on its own does not justify any means for gaining it.

The Bible also gives a moral framework for decisions about what to do with science. Naturalism does not point the way to what ought to be done; it only shows what can be done. As long as science goes forward without a moral framework, we will have more and more technology without really knowing what to do with it. We have the capacity for our own destruction—not just in a cataclysmic explosion, but little by little as the quality of life is eroded by a faster-moving society which no one can halt. Naturalism will not provide the answers.

CREATION AND CHRIST

The world is an orderly place, created by a rational creator with a purpose in mind. That purpose was to bring a redeemed people under the headship of his Son, who inherits the whole of creation. Creation was made for Jesus Christ, and also by him, the perfect ruler. As we come into relationship with Jesus we take on that perfect rule which we were made to have in him. The world was made for Christ, and as part of that, it was made habitable for us.

That means science is possible, in the sense that we can have confidence that the world will make sense and be investigable. We do not expect it to be random and unpredictable. We expect it to have an underlying order. Moreover, the Bible encourages us to understand and learn from that order. As part of the people of God, living in and appreciating his creation, it is a good thing to strive for knowledge of the world and to understand better ways of utilising it.

As we do that, we remember that the beginning of this quest for knowledge (or wisdom) is the fear of the Lord. This is the starting point which gives us confidence that the quest is possible; it is the moral map that shows us the appropriate ways of carrying out that quest; and it is the goal and endpoint, that will make sense of all we learn. By knowing and understanding God we have confidence that the world is understandable, and we are shown the appropriate way to treat our findings and each other as we learn more.

Finally, however, the Bible's attitude to science is that this quest to learn from the world will never give us the ultimate understanding of what it is all about. Our knowledge will always be limited. In the world itself, we will see evidence of orderliness and purpose, but we will not know what the purpose is. We will see the handiwork of a creator, but we will not find that creator. We will not know who the creator is, or why he created the universe, until we find him in Christ. Nor will we solve all the problems of the world by our quest for scientific knowledge. The world is inherently distorted and fallen, and will only be put right at the end of time, when God puts it right.

According to the Bible, science—or any pursuit that investigates our world—when conducted without God, is ultimately foolishness. It may come up with elements of correct knowledge, and will be useful within a limited sphere. However it will never actually give *wisdom* and will only in the end mislead the seeker. The world is there to be investigated; but what we will discover is strictly limited. Without knowledge of Christ, for whom the universe was created, we may discover lots of pieces of the puzzle, and even fit a few of them together, but we will never know what the whole picture is.

Where is the conflict between science and Christianity then? Not in the systems themselves. Science is not opposed to, neither does it disprove, the Bible; on the contrary, science needs the very philosophical tools which the Bible provides. If this is so, why are the two in conflict? Why is science pitted against Christianity?

If we are to find the source of conflict, we should not look at the two systems of thought, but rather at the people who use them.

Part III

CONFLICT

Parts I and II, taken together, leave us with an interesting conundrum. For no matter how much we stress that there need be no conflict between science and religion, there are still a great many people who see the two as being in conflict. It is the most common way for the popular media to refer to the subject. It is an assumption that is taken for granted in many people's minds. If there is no particular need for a war between science and religion, why is it that our culture has had one?

There are many dimensions to this conflict as it has actually occurred in our society. What we can aim to do here before finishing our study is to explore some aspects of the conflict which help to understand why it is there. In doing so, we may come to see that it will always be there in one way or another, for this is more than a purely intellectual matter open to philosophical resolution. It is something much more fundamental to human nature, and so will probably always be part of society at some level.

CHAPTER 9
Conflict on the public agenda

The preceding chapters would suggest that to a large extent it is basic misunderstanding and misinformation when discussing science and Christianity which put the two in conflict. A lot of the biblical information about God's action in the world is unknown in our post-biblical society, and people are ignorant about its content; while at the same time, false and rather two-dimensional images of science distort the nature of the debate as well. Unfortunately, perpetuation of such misunderstanding can happen on both 'sides'. Both Christians and scientists have been guilty of claiming ideological territories for their subject which go beyond what they can support, and so there is an unnecessary clash over boundary lines. When science becomes a metaphysical position, in which scientific explanation is the only explanation and the objects of scientific enquiry the only existing objects, then it has claimed far too much territory—more than it can sustain. Just as God is not a source of particular scientific theories, neither is science a grounds for the understanding of life and meaning.

Ignorance of what the Bible actually says about God's work in the world, and misunderstanding of the reasonable limitations of scientific explanation, create a public conflict which is to a large degree misguided. Better education in both areas would go a long way towards cooling down a highly emotional debate.

At the same time, there is an historical dimension to the conflict between science and Christianity which forms another part of the story. There is not the space here to review the entire history of the interactions between science and religious thought, nor even of science and Christianity—others have done this work in detail. What we can do is suggest some elements of the relationship which perpetuate the idea of 'conflict'.

One ongoing factor is that certain aspects of the 'warfare' have been socially and politically engineered. That is, there have been people with a particular personal viewpoint who have been in a position to spread that viewpoint widely, and have it accepted as public knowledge. At certain key points, there have been figures who have had a great deal of power over public opinion and have been particularly successful in creating this image of conflict between science and religion.

THOMAS HUXLEY

In the nineteenth century, when a great deal of the public sense of conflict between science and Christianity began, we meet someone who was a very important figure in this conflict: Thomas Henry Huxley. Huxley was a biologist who took it upon himself to defend Darwin's theory of natural selection. He did this so successfully and forcefully that he began to be called 'Darwin's Bulldog'. Darwin himself was a quiet and retiring gentleman; he preferred to stay in the peace of his country house. Huxley, on the other hand, loved a good fight and threw himself into public debate about Darwinism.

We might ask, why did he do so? It was actually not because he thought Darwin's theory of natural selection was right; in fact, Huxley had considerable doubts about the theory. However Darwin's theory was entirely naturalistic. That meant that it suited a general ideological and political battle that Huxley carried on for most of his life. This was the battle to see science—not just technical science, but science as an all-embracing naturalistic philosophy—take the place of Christianity as the dominant ideology in society. Huxley wanted scientists to be the intellectual leaders, and that meant they had to depose church leaders. He wanted scientists, as professional intellectuals, to have social power.

English science in the early nineteenth century was socially not much like it is now. Scientific activities were largely carried out by rich gentlemen who did not need to earn a living. It was associated with the aristocracy and considered an 'upper-class' activity, something with which a gentleman might fill his leisure hours. It was not a career as we think of it now; it was largely privately funded, and regarded as a hobby by many. In fact, members of the nobility could join the Royal Society without ever having studied science at all; social class was more important for involvement in science than actual scientific expertise.

This meant that science was largely amateur. It did

not require certain qualifications or degrees—in fact it was not easy to get what we would think of as a 'scientific' education. Science was arranged in a fairly haphazard way. It was something any gentleman could take up in his spare time and contribute to the body of knowledge—and many did. This included many clergy, who might (for instance) go fossil-hunting or collect geological data.

Moreover, this state of science meant that any educated gentleman could reasonably comment on science, and that naturally included church leaders. So when Darwin's theory was published, it was expected that the opinion of theologians would form part of the assessment of this new scientific theory. Many theologians had a keen interest in, and fair knowledge of, science. For instance, Bishop Wilberforce, who had a famous confrontation with Huxley over Darwin's theory, was very well-read and competent to comment on the theory.

Ambitious men like Huxley were opposed to this state of affairs in science. One aspect was the political one of who controlled science; amateurs or professionals. Science was dominated by wealthy men who could have a say in science simply because of their social position. Huxley, who like many other young men had to earn a living, was part of a rising group in the later nineteenth century that wanted science to become more professional. He and his allies sought to gain control of the scientific institutions of research and education.

Although it sounds like a conspiracy theory, this was in truth what happened. Through a network of informal contacts, a small group of scientific men managed to gain control of science in England. One remarkable group which has come to light through historical research is the 'X-club' (the name it gave itself). This group, which sounds like something out of science fiction, consisted of nine men, including Thomas Huxley, who would meet for dinner once a month just before the meetings of the Royal Society. Between themselves they decided who they wished to see in power in various scientific institutions in England. They were very successful; for instance, from 1873 to 1885 every president of the Royal Society was a member of the X-club. They also managed to have friends elected to prominent positions in other scientific societies all over England.

While this was happening behind the scenes, Huxley himself was carrying on a public battle. Huxley wanted men of science to be seen as intellectual leaders. He wished to see science itself have intellectual independence; in particular, to be free from religious opinion. It was a battle for who had the right to say what was true. Huxley wanted this right to be restricted to scientists; he did not want theologians to have that right. He did not try to abolish religion altogether, but he wanted it to be reduced to a matter of feeling, not intellect, and he wanted it to lose control of education and public opinion. In the arena of knowledge and thought—matters of truth and reality—science had to be the leader. There is only one kind of knowledge, he insisted, and one way of acquiring it; the scientific way. His commitment to scientific naturalism was, in fact, almost a new religion. There were certainly many quasi-religious elements to Huxley's thought. He would speak of the 'church scientific', with himself as a bishop and his lectures 'lay sermons'.

Huxley championed science against theology, and insisted on the superiority of science. He and his friends publicised and popularised the successes of scientific method; the improvements in industry, for instance. What Huxley was proclaiming, however, was not merely science as an activity but as a naturalistic philosophy. The success of science as an activity was used to defend science as philosophy. Huxley did not merely want scientific technique and knowledge taught; he wished naturalism to become the dominant ideology in society— and for theology to lose its place amongst intellectual leadership.

Huxley's main technique for doing this was to state constantly that science and theology were opposed to each other, and that in this battle, science won. Huxley would portray the relationship between science and religion as a struggle comparable to the great battles of mythology. He compared theologians to the strangled snakes lying around the cradle of Hercules, and claimed that science would inevitably triumph over religion. Christian orthodoxy, when pitted against science, always had to retire "bleeding and crushed". Scientists had far greater resources, as "The majesty of Fact is on their side". With this kind of rhetoric, Huxley presented science as a great force of progress marching forward, constantly opposed by Christianity but inevitably triumphant. Huxley was a very powerful public speaker, as well as being a popular writer. Moreover, he spent most of his professional life engaged in public debates. In time, people began to believe him. The idea that science was actually in conflict with theology began to be more widespread.

WHITE AND DRAPER: THE CONFLICT CONTINUES

When two works were published later in the nineteenth century that dealt with the relationship between science and religion, Christianity became more firmly established as the 'enemy' of science. These works were John Draper's *History of the Conflict between Religion and Science*, and Andrew Dickson White's *A History of the Warfare of Science with Theology in Christendom*, which gave voice to the bitterness that each of the men felt for established religion, arising from their life experiences.

John William Draper (1811-1882) was a professor of chemistry in New York when he was asked to write a popular history of science and religion. He had also published in history, so he seemed an ideal choice for the job. Draper had some religious belief, it seems, that dwindled over the course of his life. However his history of science and religion, *History of the Conflict between Religion and Science*, reveals in its title what he thought of the relationship between the two. "The history of Science is not a mere record of isolated discoveries", he wrote; "it is a narrative of the conflict of two contending powers, the expansive force of the human intellect on one side, and the compression arising from traditionary faith and human interests on the other".[1] In fact, Draper's book was a vehement attack on the Catholic

---

1. John William Draper, *History of the Conflict between Science and Religion*, Kegan Paul, Trench and Co., London, 1883, p. vi.

Church. It was not a history so much as an expression of his own reaction to Catholic pronouncements, and of his conviction that Christianity (although by this he meant Catholicism) was absolutely incompatible with science. As history it was, by any standards, very poor. However the sentiment it expressed became very powerful. The book was a massive success, translated into ten languages and going through multiple editions in the United States and Great Britain. The idea of 'conflict' between science and religion had gripped the public mind.

Similar literature followed, but one work which was particularly influential was by Andrew Dickson White. He grew up in a High Church Episcopalian family, but began to resent his upbringing when the 'Christian' university his father insisted on him attending turned out to be a place of dissipation and carousing. He left for Yale, under his father's disapproval, and studied further at the Sorbonne and the University of Berlin. His first position as a professor of history was at the University of Michigan, where the president was attempting to build a non-sectarian university, but was facing considerable opposition from the religious colleges. White sympathized with the president and began to dream of establishing his own university. He was elected to the State Senate of New York in 1863 and persuaded the wealthy philanthropist Ezra Cornell, a fellow-senator, to provide funds. The bill was vehemently opposed by the local denominational colleges, and the secular press were drawn in. However the university went ahead.

White was considerably angered by the attacks made on his university, and eventually hit back with a lecture in New York that used historical examples of conflict between science and religion to show that science always emerged victorious. The lecture was printed in full, and widely republished. White eventually expanded it into a book, *The Warfare of Science,* which was very popular. White became a crusader against his religious enemies. Finally, in 1896, he published the two-volume *A History of the Warfare of Science with Theology in Christendom.* The theme is familiar:

> In all modern history, interference with science in the supposed interest of religion, no matter how conscientious such interference may have been, has resulted in the direst evils both to religion and to science, and invariable; and on the other hand, all untrammelled scientific investigation, no matter how dangerous to religion some of its states may have seemed for the time to be, has invariably resulted in the highest good of both of religion and of science.[2]

The historian White wrote a far better book than Draper. Moreover White was not trying to enforce a war, and indeed insisted that he greatly admired many clergy. White did not claim that science and religion were inherently enemies. Rather, he argued that people had only too often attempted to defend religion in a way that was actually detrimental to the pursuit of truth, and what was best

---

2. Andrew Dickson White, *A History of the Warfare of Science with Theology in Christendom,* Dover Publications Inc, New York, 1960, p. viii.

for society. He was not so much attacking religion as making an exasperated outburst against those people who would obstruct, in the name of religion, what he saw to be work for the good of mankind.

However, this was not what the public heard from his book: instead, it was seen to declare science and religion irreconcilable enemies. The effect of Draper's work was to make the conflict even more bitter. The notion that, historically, science and theology had always been in conflict, became accepted as fact. It was used not only by those who wished to attack Christianity, but began to be commonplace in textbooks and academic literature. Even though a great deal of more recent historical research has shown the idea to be very misleading, the idea continues.

This opposition between science and Christianity occurred at a time when new techniques of historical criticism, which were thought to be 'scientific', were throwing doubt upon the historical validity of the Bible. New critiques of the life of Jesus, such as Strauss' *Life of Jesus*, claimed that many elements of the Gospels were mythological, pious inventions or delusions of later Christians which had been added to the bare historical basis of the story. That historical basis appeared to become more and more flimsy as historical criticism claimed to strip the Gospel accounts of historical credibility. Such historical critiques, now for the most part thoroughly discarded in scholarly circles, at the time shook the confidence that many had in their Bibles. If science and Christianity were at war, it did indeed seem that science would win.

The dominance of a new naturalistic and scientific world view in opposition to Christian orthodoxy gained prominence in public discourse with surprising vigour. Scientists championed naturalism to the extent that less dogmatic colleagues protested at their evangelistic zeal for their religion. The movement supported so fiercely by Huxley and his fellow naturalistic science enthusiasts was very effective. It was no accident that Huxley was also prominent in publishing; he was amongst those who founded the journal *Nature*, now one of the leading scientific journals, but in part established to promote Huxley's particular view of science.

HUXLEY'S VICTORY

If Huxley's aim was to see science dominant in education, and naturalism take public intellectual leadership, it can only be said that he succeeded. The prestige attached to scientific authority, which perhaps hit its peak a few decades ago, is still immense. Scientific opinion carries great weight in a huge number of social issues, and disciplines wishing for greater prestige try to establish themselves as sciences. Science subjects in schools are regarded as the 'hardest' and therefore the domain of the elite. Huxley's dream of seeing a society in which scientific opinion carries great authority in intellectual discussion, while theological opinion is marginalized, has become reality.

Huxley's aim to see science and Christianity established as enemies has largely succeeded as well. It is by far the most common metaphor for discussion of science and Christianity, and even those discussions which come to an alternative conclusion will start with the popular 'conflict' idea as a popularly accepted and recognizable image. This is by no means just a surface image, either; it is not at all uncommon to see letters to editors in newspapers or science magazines, protesting against promotion of religious ideas as 'unscientific'.

This image, however, is surprisingly in contradiction to the sheer numbers of religious believers within the sciences. A recent survey of religious belief amongst scientists in the United States (published in the journal Huxley helped found, *Nature*) showed that forty percent of scientists asserted a personal belief in a personal God—almost exactly the same percentage as when a similar survey was conducted in 1916. Those actually doing science, the intellectuals themselves, are not over-whelmingly anti-Christian and a significant percentage do not see a conflict between religious belief and scientific work. The conflict metaphor is not appropriate for a large part of the professional scientific community.

Amongst science popularisers, however, we have a different story. Science writer Richard Dawkins is famous for his outright dismissals of any kind of religious belief:

> Science shares with religion the claim that it answers deep questions about origins, the nature of life, and the cosmos, but there the resemblance ends. Scientific beliefs are supported by evidence, and they get results. Myths and faiths are not and do not.[3]

---

3. Richard Dawkins, *River out of Eden: A Darwinian View of Life*, Weidenfeld and Nicolson, London, 1995, p. 33.

It is a classically stark contrast: the true and the false, the useful and the useless. The two are rivals but one hopelessly outclasses the other.

This suggests that the real 'enemy' of Christianity is not science at all, but science writers. It is these highly prominent publicists of science who propagate the 'warfare' image, even though the warfare is not actually in evidence in the two systems of ideas or in a very large number of individual minds. Of course there are many writers and publishers of popular books who are both scientists and believers in some kind of religious faith, including orthodox Christianity, but none attain the media dominance of the few highly influential secularists. The science and religion 'warfare' idea is a peculiarly strong one, which is apparently not to be shaken by evidence to the contrary.

This evidence to the contrary—the fact that there are so many scientists who also profess a personal faith in God—emphasizes a further popular misrepresentation of the relationship, but one more subtle. That is, we speak of 'science' and 'religion' as if they are two opposing camps, two bodies or institutions which exist independently; however as we have seen, they are *people*, and they are frequently one and the same person. Many people are interested in finding out the truth about the world. No-one can claim that right exclusively to him or herself. Although it is a convenient shorthand— a shorthand made use of in this book—we must never forget that 'science' does not *do* anything; *people* do things, and the same person may both investigate the world, and know God.

When we embody science, we fall into the trap of thinking of 'it' as a being to which we must have certain attitudes. Perhaps we are smugly confident in this being, thinking that it will provide us with all answers about life. Perhaps we are afraid of this being, as something which might destroy our faith. Either attitude makes the mistake of turning the activity of people into an entity of its own. However, when we think of science as an activity, which (in principle) anyone can do, then both the smugness and the fear lose their basis. We can start to talk about how we make sense of life with all the resources available to us.

Science and Christianity are not in conflict, or at least need not be. We have been made to think otherwise by people who have taken an aggressive position and created conflict. Because certain *people* wanted naturalistic science to gain social authority, we have been made to think that the *ideas* of science and Christianity are in conflict—but indeed they are not. As many individual scientists show, as well as many people outside professional science who simply have an interest in the ideas, Christianity and science are very compatible. Our study of what science is, and how the Bible relates to it, demonstrates that these people are not deluded. The idea that believing the Bible and believing in science are incompatible—"leave your brains at the church door"—is an idea that has been *taught* to us. We are justified in questioning it.

CHAPTER 10

Unnatural enemies

We have pointed to some of the social elements in the supposed conflict between science and Christianity, the deliberate engineering of a public image by determined propagandists. This is certainly an element which needs to be understood. It needs to be made clear that the debate is not simply one of ideologies but has a higher level of competing interests.

However, a deeper issue remains to be addressed. Understanding the role of social engineering does not fully answer the question. If we step back still further, we notice that discussion about the proper relationship between human knowledge and philosophy, and the knowledge of God revealed in Christianity, goes back a long way before the nineteenth century. The clash may have been less violent, and its public face more controlled, but since the early days of Christianity the questions have certainly been asked. There has always been an uneasy tension between human philosophies of understanding the natural world, and Christian belief.

Even though the scientific method and biblical reve-

lation in essence are not in conflict, people often are and
have been for centuries. It has happened that religious
institutions have condemned particular lines of scientific
research; and it has happened that scientific establish-
ments have marginalised religious belief. It has happened
that religious writers have cursorily rejected scientific
theories; and scientific writers have cursorily dismissed
religious doctrine. Misunderstandings and inflated claims
have been made on both sides.

In the end, however, the underlying reasons for the
continued conflict lie in the human soul, not in abstract
matters of metaphysics.

One reason is simple arrogance. Humans have the
almost inevitable tendency to think that they are right,
and opponents wrong, and to be quite vocal about it.
Dogmatic arrogance is the mark of the human race
generally, regardless of the ideological camp, and it
breeds conflict. Since last century, the free thinkers and
now the science popularists have commonly complained
of the arrogance of religious dogmatism, the inflexibility
of revelation which sets down the truth and allows no
other viewpoints. However, theological writers have also
pointed out that science writers wish to claim the ground
both of science and theology for themselves, and not
allow theologians their say. Both sides have fought for
intellectual ground, and accused the other of arrogance.

Yet surely, we would like to think, an intelligent
discussion is possible. Surely throughout the centuries
some enlightened thinkers have risen above arrogance
and seen the issues more clearly. Certainly there have
been some gentle and worthy writers who did not seek

conflict, but they have been the exception rather the rule.

In the end, there is a part of all of us that *wants* science to be in conflict with God. We are all the children of Adam and Eve. We would all prefer to dispense with God, if that were possible. We *want* science's answers to be good enough to contend with God's answers, or render them obsolete. As long as there is a conflict, and science has the upper hand, then perhaps we might be able to do away with God; or at least we can feel that God depends on our rationality rather than us depending on his revelation. We would so much rather work it out for ourselves. We would like to be able to observe, and reason, and come up with the ultimate answers; for we have a lot of confidence in our own powers of reasoning. To have to trust that God is the only one who gives the ultimate answers is rather belittling. It does not sit well with our pride as human beings.

There is a conflict between science and Christianity, for there is a conflict between humanity and God. It starts with Adam and Eve, but that is only the start. The story of humanity is the story of our rebellion against God and his ways. Rather than ruling the world as his representatives, as his vice-regents, we want to displace God, and run things our own way.

The Tower of Babel is a potent symbol of this. The story is told in Genesis 11:

> Now the whole world had one language and a common speech. As men moved eastward, they found a plain in Shinar and settled there. They said to each other, "Come, let's make bricks and bake

them thoroughly". They used brick instead of stone, and bitumen for mortar. Then they said, "Come, let us build ourselves a city, with a tower that reaches to the heavens, so that we may make a name for ourselves and not be scattered over the face of the whole earth". But the Lord came down to see the city and the tower that the men were building. The Lord said, "If as one people speaking the same language they have begun to do this, then nothing they plan to do will be impossible for them. Come, let us go down and confuse their language so they will not understand each other." So the Lord scattered them from there over all the earth, and they stopped building the city. That is why it was called Babel—because there the Lord confused the language of the whole world. From there the Lord scattered them over the face of the whole earth (Genesis 11:1-9).

This is a story of humanity trying to build, through its own cooperation and ingenuity, a challenge to heaven. We are still trying to do it. Instead of seeing science as the noble pursuit that it is, investigating God's world, we try to make it our means of becoming god ourselves. And because we are very good at science, we feel some measure of confidence that one day, ultimately, we will succeed. In the meantime, we do not like being reminded that God will not be challenged.

The Tower of Babel warns us that we will not become God. For all our mastery of the world, we will always fail to cooperate sufficiently to create the name we crave. We can discover the genetic and social sources of bad behaviour, but we cannot make people behave well. We can analyse the dreadful effects of pollution and over-production on our environment, but we cannot make governments cooperate. We can do so much, but there remains so much we cannot do. Yet this is hard to admit; for admitting it is tantamount to admitting that we are not really in control, and that Someone else is.

No matter how clever we are, we will not be a challenge to God and neither will our activities; if we think they can be, we delude ourselves. God, in his wisdom, has created an intricate, habitable and investigable world. It is our privilege to study it.

References and further reading

A book like this covers areas which on their own have literally hundreds of texts about them, so it is difficult to find a way of adequately referencing the ideas without swamping the reader with information. I have therefore tried here to suggest starting points in the literature which will provide further bibliographies for readers who wish to take this matter further, as well as referencing specific publications I have referred to in the text of the book.

Part 1

An excellent introduction to the historical origins of science is Steven Shapin's *The Scientific Revolution*, The University of Chicago Press, London, 1996. His bibliography offers a way into the immense amount of literature on the history of science. Francis Bacon's writings are available in many editions; for the ideas mentioned in chapter 1, see in particular *The New Organon*, *New Atlantis* and *Advancement of Learning*.

For an introduction to issues in the philosophy of science, try Alan Chalmers *What is this thing called Science?: An assessment of the nature and status of science and its methods*, University of Queensland Press, St Lucia, London and New York, 1982. More technical discussions can be found in useful collections such as Frederick Suppe (ed.), *The Structure of Scientific Theories*, University of Illinois Press, Urbana and Chicago, 1977 (including a superb critical introduction by Suppe which surveys the twentieth-century field up to that point); or more recently David Papineau (ed), *The Philosophy of Science*, Oxford University Press, Oxford, 1996. David Hume's argument about induction, mentioned in chapter 2, is found in *A Treatise of Human Nature*. Thomas Kuhn's ideas about paradigms are explained in *The Structure of Scientific Revolutions*, University of Chicago Press, Chicago, 1962 (for critiques of his argument, see the volume edited by Suppe above). For an introduction to the discussion of the theory-ladenness of observation, see N. R. Hanson, *Patterns of Discovery*, Cambridge University Press, Cambridge, 1958.

One of the best ways to keep up with the current content of scientific knowledge is through a magazine like *New Scientist*, published weekly; *New Scientist* also publishes summaries of different aspects of science. For comment on the Mars discoveries, see David Sinclair, 'Life on Mars...really?', *kategoria*, 1996, *number 3*, pp. 51-55. The research paper which announced the possibility of life on Mars was D. S. McKay *et al*, 'Search for past life on Mars: possible relic biogenic activity in Martian meteorite ALH84001', *Science*, 1996, *273*, pp. 924-930; further discussion can be followed in *New Scientist*, 21-28 December 1996.

The books referred to which use religious imagery in scientific writing were Richard Dawkins, *River out of Eden: A Darwinian View of Life*, Weidenfeld and Nicolson, London, 1995, and Stuart Kauffman, *At Home in the Universe: The Search for Laws of Self-Organization and Complexity*, Viking, London, 1995.

Part 2

Only one book should really be referenced here: the Bible. It is worth the trouble to look up all the quoted verses and read them in context, to gain an accurate picture of what the text is saying.

For further reading, however, parts of various books are useful. J. I. Packer's *Knowing God*, Hodder and Stoughton, London, 1973 is a classic in the theology of God and his activity. Other useful references are the sections on creation in T. C. Hammond, *In Understanding be Men: A Handbook of Christian Doctrine*, Inter-varsity Press, Leicester, 1968, and Bruce Milne, *Know the Truth: A Handbook of Christian Belief*, Inter-Varsity Press, Leicester, 1982. Also, as in so many areas of theology, little has surpassed John Calvin, *Institutes of the Christian Religion*, The Westminster Press, Philadelphia, 1960.

An introduction to biblical theology is found in Graeme Goldsworthy's *Gospel and Kingdom: A Christian Interpretation of the Old Testament*, The Paternoster Press, Exeter, 1981 and *According to Plan: The Unfolding Revelation of God in the Bible*, Inter-varsity Press, Leicester, 1991. Also essential reading on the topic of wisdom in the Old Testament is his *Gospel and Wisdom: Israel's Wisdom Literature in the Christian Life*, Paternoster Press, Carlisle, 1987 and 1995.

Part 3

Probably the best place to start for the historical interactions between science and Christianity is with John Hedley Brooke's *Science and Religion: Some Historical Perspectives*, Cambridge University Press, Cambridge, 1991. Another useful volume is David C. Lindberg and Ronald L. Numbers (eds), *God and Nature: Historical Essays on the Encounter between Christianity and Science*, University of California Press, Berkeley, Los Angeles and London, 1986. For Thomas Huxley's life and political manoeuvres, see David Starling, 'Thomas Huxley and the 'warfare' between science and religion: mythology, politics and ideology', *kategoria*, 1996, *number 3*, pp. 33-50; also Colin A. Russell, 'The conflict metaphor and its social origins', *Science and Christian Belief*, 1989, *1*, pp. 3-26; J. Vernon Jensen 'The X club: fraternity of Victorian scientists', *The British Journal for the History of Science*, 1970, *5*, pp. 63-72; Roy M. MacLeod, 'The X-club: a social network of science in late-Victorian England', *Notes and Records of The Royal Society of London*, 1970, *24*, pp. 305-322; Edward Caudill, 'The Bishop-Eaters: the publicity campaign for Darwin and *On the Origin of Species*', *Journal of the History of Ideas*, 1994, *55*, pp. 441-466; and Ruth Barton 'Evolution: the Whitworth Gun in Huxley's war for the liberation of science from theology', in David Oldroyd and Ian Langham (eds), *The Wider Domain of Evolutionary Thought*, D. Reidel

Publishing Company, Dordrecht, Boston and London, 1983, pp. 261-287. Also very useful is James R. Moore, *The Post-Darwinian Controversies: A Study of the Protestant Struggle to come to terms with Darwin in Great Britain and America 1870-1900*, Cambridge University Press, Cambridge, 1979.

Quotation was made of Richard Dawkins *River Out of Eden*, as cited above. The paper mentioned on religious belief amongst scientists was Edward J. Larson and Larry Witham, 'Scientists are still keeping the faith', *Nature*, 1997, *386*, pp. 435-436.